THE REVOLT AGAINST
THE CHURCH

IS VOLUME

78

OF THE

Twentieth Century Encyclopedia of Catholicism

UNDER SECTION

VII

THE HISTORY OF THE CHURCH

IT IS ALSO THE

88TH

VOLUME IN ORDER OF PUBLICATION

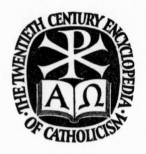

Edited by *HENRI DANIEL-ROPS* of the *Académie Française*

THE REVOLT AGAINST
THE CHURCH

By LÉON CRISTIANI

Translated from the French by R. F. TREVETT

HAWTHORN BOOKS · PUBLISHERS · *New York*

230.2
T97
v.78

First Edition, June, 1962

CONTENTS

CHAPTER I

THE PAPACY FROM 1450

TO 1492

THE JUBILEE OF 1450

The period of the Church's history which we are to survey in
the present book opens with a "golden year" as the phrase
went at the time. This period extends from 1450 to 1623. It is
difficult for us to imagine the emotion which shook the whole
of Christendom in the course of the year 1449 when it was
known that Pope Nicholas V had decreed that the year 1450
should be that of the universal Jubilee, a *holy year* as we say
today. Christendom had just passed through difficult times.
After the "Babylonian Captivity" (the term used to describe
the period of the popes' residence at Avignon from 1305 to
1378), the Great Schism had broken out. Then, when this
terrible scandal had been eliminated in its turn, a regrettable
conflict had arisen between the pope and the Council of Basle.
It had lasted for eighteen years. A new schism had followed.
But shortly after the accession of Nicholas V in 1447, peace
had gradually returned. The new pope had shown rare breadth
of mind. The dissidents had submitted to his authority. The
antipope (the last of his kind), Felix V, had done likewise.

It was announced that the "golden year" would begin at
Christmas 1449 and would end the following Christmas.√
Nicholas V went in person to the opening of the Holy Door
at St John Lateran. Pilgrims began immediately to flow in

from all sides. The chroniclers of the time have left abundant accounts which abound in picturesque descriptions. "From every European country", writes Ludwig Pastor the historian of the popes, "pilgrims came and they were of every condition and age: Italians and those from beyond the mountains, men and women, young and old, the healthy and the sick. With their long pilgrim's staff in their hand and the broad hat decorated with shells hanging from their shoulders, they came down the great highways, singing their hymns and reciting their prayers."

And Rome really seemed the centre of the world, the capital city of men's faith and hope. The thought of gaining a plenary indulgence (not often granted in those days) filled all hearts with joy. Even the convents opened their doors to allow their monks and nuns to make the journey. So universal and powerful was the movement that some religious wondered whether it was necessary to obtain their superiors' permission in order to set out. This delicate point had to be decided. And the famous cardinal, Nicholas of Cusa, was obliged to declare in the pope's name that "obedience is of greater value than the indulgence".

One of the most splendid days of the Holy Year was that on which the celebrated preacher Bernardine of Siena was canonized. He had died in 1444, six years before, and was already universally honoured. The ceremony took place on the feast of Pentecost, May 24th, 1450. The procession set out from the great house of the Franciscans, Ara Coeli, and numbered 3,000 friars. Among them celebrated preachers were to be seen. Some of these were also to be canonized at a later date: John Capistran, James of the March and others. Among the crowds of pilgrims was a great saint, Rita of Cascia, the stigmatic.

This enthusiasm, this great gathering of pilgrims from every country, the splendour of the religious feasts, paint a picture of a whole epoch for us. There was a vigorous Christian faith. The dark shadows we shall have to point out had hardly yet begun to appear. And another characteristic sign of the times were the tragic episodes which marked the Holy Year. When the first warm weather came, Rome began to be a plague spot. An epidemic broke out. The pope was obliged to leave the city on June 18th, thus interrupting the Jubilee which was only resumed on October 25th. At that date, the pilgrims arrived in as great numbers as before and this was in fact the cause of a terrible accident. One day in December, there was such a rush on the St Angelo Bridge that large numbers of pilgrims were thrown into the Tiber and two or three hundred of them perished. The prestige of Rome and of the papacy did not suffer as a result. What happened to this prestige shortly after, we are now about to see.

NICHOLAS V (1447–55)

Nicholas V, as we have said, had become pope in 1447. His election on March 6th of that year had caused universal amazement, but people soon came to the conclusion that the choice had been providential. Thomas Parentucelli was of very humble origin. He was born in 1397 and was the son of a doctor in the town of Sarzana. He was an orphan at an early age but had been able to continue his education until he eventually took a post as tutor in Florence. While still young, he had consorted with the men who were already beginning to be called "humanists" or, as we should now say, "men of letters". He became a priest and entered the service of the devout Cardinal Nicholas of Albergati to whom he rendered devoted service for twenty-three years until 1443. His devotion and zeal were rewarded. In the course of three years he had become successively a bishop (1444), a cardinal (1446) and pope.

He was a man of puny appearance, thin and ugly with sparkling, humorous black eyes. Though labouring under the burden of ugliness, yet he was devoted to the beautiful. Men recognized in him every quality and virtue, piety, wisdom,

knowledge, goodness, generosity. He also had his faults:
he was impetuous, headstrong and impatient. But he was
upright, frank and an enemy of flattery of every kind. He was
perhaps a little too conscious of his own kindness of heart.
He was known to accompany a gift with the words: "Take
it. You won't always have a Nicholas with you."

His pontificate marks a turning-point in papal history.
It has often been said that he was the first of the Renaissance
popes. Aeneas Sylvius, the subtle writer who was to be the
next pope but one, said of him: "He knows everything, the
philosophers, the poets, the historians, the cosmographers
and the theologians." In actual fact, he was devoid of all
personal originality in literature or art but he possessed a
remarkable and universal receptivity. Above all, he loved
books. He used part of the immense gifts he received on the
occasion of the Jubilee to collect manuscripts with which to
enrich the Vatican Library. Before his time, under Eugenius IV in 1443, the number of manuscripts amounted to no
more than 350, two of which were Greek. When he died,
there were 1,209—795 Latin and 414 Greek. It must be remembered that printing was only just beginning its career in
a very humble way in Germany.

But Nicholas V was not only the leading bibliophile of his
time, he had made up his mind to be the patron of all the
arts. The writers or [humanists] were undoubtedly his favour-
ites. He showed himself somewhat lacking in discrimination,
however, for all these men were far from being equally
estimable. Nicholas V raised the cult of beauty to the level
of high policy. He openly professed the belief that beauty is
the greatest act of homage that can be offered to God and
that the most splendid ornament of the Christian religion is
and ought to be the magnificence of its buildings, the grandeur
of its ceremonies, the sumptuousness of its setting and the
employment of all the arts in the service of God. He wanted to
make Rome the capital city of all the beautiful works of
men's hands as well as the home of the Muses. As he saw it,

the faith of the ignorant and the humble ought to be strengthened by the knowledge of the learned and the inventive power of the artists. On his death-bed he openly declared his intentions in this respect although he had not been able completely to fulfil them. We shall point out later the illusory nature of part at least of this grandiose dream. But even at the time two questions could be asked. In the first place, would the men of learning and the artists agree to put their minds and will at the service of God and for the benefit of the faith of the humble? And secondly, would the course of events allow the Church sufficient liberty and peace to accomplish her great task of salvation and the promotion of Christian civilization?

Two great dangers threatened what was still called Christendom: internal dissension and Islam's ambitions for conquest. Nicholas V had an excellent scheme to meet the first peril. He would take advantage of the renewed prestige of the papacy in order to send to the various Christian countries legates whose duty it would be to maintain or to re-establish peace and to further the cause of religious reform. This plan does great honour to Nicholas V. If his example had been followed, if the reform of the Church could have continued by means of the papal legates, it seems likely that the course of history would have been changed. Nevertheless, his choice of legates was not always equally fortunate. While men like Cardinal Nicholas of Cusa and the great preacher St John Capistran achieved remarkable results in the countries they visited, namely, Germany and Hungary, in France the ostentatious Cardinal d'Estouteville did little more than dazzle his contemporaries by his excessive display and his gifts to churches. He had no genuine influence on morals and failed to correct the too numerous abuses which afflicted society at the time.

Further there were many countries other than those we have just mentioned which were not visited at all by papal legates with the task of introducing the reform. Italy itself, as it were under the pope's very eyes, was by no means the united and brotherly land it should have been. On the contrary, between one principality and another, between one domain and another, emulation, hostility, and rivalry were constantly arising and disappearing, and the picture we shall have to sketch of private and public morals at the time will give a far from edifying idea of the Christian world during this century, however vigorously the faith endured, as the 1450 Jubilee had shown.

The peril from without was still more formidable. In any case it was increased by the fact of the divisions in the Christian countries. If we today talk of the Communist peril facing Christendom and all free countries, the fifteenth century had its "Turkish peril".

The Eastern Empire had asked for the help of the West against the threat of Islam, but in vain. It was also in vain that the Greek Church had agreed (with great difficulty and grudgingly) to bring about the "reunion of the Churches" at the Council of Ferrara and Florence (1439–45). In 1451, Murad II died. He was a sultan who had shaken Europe. His successor was a young man of twenty-one. Under the very significant name of Mohammed II he was to prove more dangerous still. In the early days of April 1453, it was learned that the city of Constantinople, the last bulwark of the Christian faith in the East, was enduring a siege to the death. Had it not been for the divisions among the Latins it is possible that the old crusading spirit might have awakened again at the last moment and have saved the city. But nothing of the kind occurred. The city was defended with great courage but the attack could not be resisted. On May 29th, 1453, Byzantium fell. For three whole days it was given over to pillage and all the horrors of defeat. Throughout the Latin Church there was a sudden wave of genuine dismay and a desire for revenge. The pope sent his legates everywhere to summon the Christian princes to a holy war. The idea was toyed with, promises were made and there was much brave talk. But the idea of the Crusade had passed away. As we shall see, it survived in the popes. It found no echo worth the name among the princes at the time, still less in the mercantile republics such as Venice and Genoa. Only a handful of heroes whom we shall see in action during the next pontificate succeeded in saving the honour of the West.

CALLISTUS III (1455–8)

The last years of Nicholas V had been made sombre by the absurd plot headed by Stephen Porcaro who had taken up arms against the pope on the strength of a bogus hankering after the ancient Roman Republic. In spite of his gentle nature, the pope had had to resort to severe measures. After an initial pardon, Stephen Porcaro was eventually hanged. The pope was deeply grieved by this execution and still more by the undercurrents of criticism it had aroused, among the general public. The year 1453, in which both Porcaro's conspiracy and also the fall of Byzantium took place, struck the pope a mortal blow. He suffered agonies from gout. His last months were marked by terrible physical and mental suffering. He died during the night of March 24th and 25th, 1455.

On April 8th, the conclave, divided as it was between two rival factions, the Colonna versus the Orsini, chose as his successor Alonso de Borja, whom the Italians called Alfonso de *Borgia*. He was a Spaniard and he took the name of Callistus III. No one could have foreseen such a choice, except perhaps the pope himself since, many years before, when he was a young priest, Vincent Ferrer, the missionary of the masses, who had died in 1419, had told him he would be elected. This explains why one of this pontiff's first acts was the canonization of the famous Dominican preacher on June 29th, 1455.

Callistus III came of vigorous stock. He was born in 1378 and ascended the throne of Peter at the age of seventy-seven. The Italians were very dissatisfied by his election. As a result he surrounded himself with Spaniards. His great qualities were admitted. He was devout, upright, prudent, a man of experience in public affairs and a learned canonist. In spite of his great age, he immediately plunged into activity. The proof of this lies in the forty-eight volumes of his *Acta*. Yet he only ruled the Church for three years.

He was a man of one idea—the Crusade. His single ambition was to save Christendom from the Turkish peril. As a Spaniard, he had the Crusade in his blood. Immediately after his election, he made a solemn vow to the Blessed Trinity that he would devote all the wealth of the Church and, if necessary, give his own life in order to drive back the Turks and recapture Constantinople. This vow was announced in writing to almost every European country and raised high hopes in many breasts.

In an attempt to carry out his plan, he promulgated the Bull of the Crusade as early as May 15th, 1455. In it he renewed all the spiritual favours and indulgences already granted by Nicholas V on September 30th, 1453 to all who took part in the war against the Turks. Legates were sent at once to the various nations, the indefatigable Carvajal to Germany, Poland and Hungary, Nicholas of Cusa to England and Cardinal Alain to France. The Franciscans were given the special task of preaching the Crusade everywhere. But the Dominicans and Augustinians also took their share of the work. Subsidies were raised for the war against the Turks. Bogus collectors were responsible for certain abuses in this connection. The pope sold all he could of the Church's treasures. The humanists even accused him of selling books (manuscripts) from the Vatican Library. In actual fact, he sold five of these and they were of secondary importance. In his view, everything was of secondary importance when compared with the Crusade. A fleet had to be built. The pope set about it with all the power at his command. He was assisted by Cardinal Scarampo, one of those prelates of other days who were men of war more often than men of God.

But while the pontiff was thus bending all his energies to

the task, the princes made no move. They were jealous of one another and absorbed by their little local ambitions and intrigues. They thought far more of despoiling each other than of fighting the Turks. While the pope was selling his salt-cellars and declaring he would make do with a linen mitre, the princes held on to their money or only parted with it in small sums. Meanwhile the enemy was advancing. Mohammed wanted to crush Hungary. In June 1456 he marched towards the Danube and laid siege to Belgrade. The city was subjected to violent bombardment. It was considered the last bulwark of the Christian world. Three men, known as the three "Johns" (Aeneas Sylvius), Cardinal John de Carvajal, the preacher John Capistran and the military hero John Hunyadi, rushed to the spot. The blockade of Belgrade was broken and the city supplied with provisions on July 14th, 1456. A week later, Mohammed II launched an attack which he intended to be decisive. The pope had issued a Bull on June 29th, inviting all Christians to prayer. He had instituted the evening Angelus as a special prayer for the war against the Turks. All these prayers and efforts were crowned with success. The Moslems were defeated and Mohammed, who had taken part in the battle, scimitar in hand, was himself wounded and obliged to give the order to retreat. The Turkish camp with all its arms and baggage and a portion of its artillery remained in the hands of the Christians. The date was July 21st, 1456. Christian Europe breathed again. John Capistran in his enthusiasm proclaimed that the general defeat of the Moslems would soon follow. But John Hunyadi died on August 11th, and on the 23rd John Capistran followed him at the age of seventy-one. Hopes grew dim again. The pope instituted the feast of the Transfiguration to be celebrated on August 6th in commemoration of the memorable victory of Belgrade. The pope's one great consolation after the deaths of John Capistran and John Hunyadi was the fact that there still remained in the person of George Castriota, prince of Albania and better known by the famous name of Scanderbeg, a hero to whom he gave the official title of "Soldier of Christ".

Callistus died, without having been able to fulfil his vow, on August 6th, 1458, the feast of the Transfiguration which he had himself instituted. We should have nothing but praise for him if there had not been one blot on his pontificate which we can never cease to deplore. He was too fond of his own family. He carried nepotism to lamentable lengths. He had a large number of relatives, nephews of striking appearance, of vigorous and hardy stock, but almost all ambitious and prone to the pleasures of the flesh. This excellent pope certainly did not suspect that one of these nephews, the brilliant Rodrigo Borgia, was to bring disgrace on his family and the Church.

PIUS II (1458–64)

Eighteen cardinals attended the conclave which opened on August 16th, 1458. Cardinal Capranica, who might well have obtained the majority needed for election as pope, had died two days previously. On August 19th, the cardinals chose Cardinal Piccolomini (Aeneas Sylvius). He took the name of Pius II. He was fifty-three, but already an old man, suffering from gout (then very frequent), gall-stones and an almost ceaseless cough. Still more than Nicholas V he could be called a humanist pope. He was born at Corsignano near Siena. His youth had been stormy and it was with some hesitation that he had considered the obligations of the Christian priesthood. He had rapidly shown himself to be a writer, poet, orator and diplomat and anxious to offer his services to the party which seemed the more popular, first the conciliar party, then the papal. As he grew older and as the papacy won its victory, his ideas had become more settled. Once he had become pope, he took care to issue a Bull forbidding any appeal from the pope to the Council. But this did not prevent these appeals from recurring on very many occasions. As a pope, Pius II deserves nothing but praise. He was simple in his habits, thrifty, zealous, devout and had a special devotion to our Lady. As one of the principal humanists, he had a love of nature and a predilection for forests and fields. He has left us a *Description of the World* which he did not have time to revise but which places him in the front rank of the geographers and cosmographers of his century. Towards the end of his life he wrote his *Commentaries*, that is, his memoirs, and they are one of the most valuable sources for the history of the period.

In the political sphere, Pius II continued the struggle against the Turks with energy and resolution. He encountered the same obstacles, and the same failure of the Europeans to understand the issue, as Callistus III had done.

He held a Congress of the Powers at Mantua to launch the Crusade. Few attended it. Pius II made a superb speech which is still extant. But it was no use his invoking the great figures of Godfrey of Bouillon, Baldwin, Bohemund, Tancred and of all those who had once delivered Jerusalem. It was no use his wishing to devote his own strength and even to give his life for the triumph of the Cross over Islam. It was no use his attempting to levy a tax on accumulated wealth in order to finance the Crusade. He asked the clergy for a tenth of their revenues, the Jews for a twentieth, the laity for a thirtieth. But he was answered with nothing but lukewarmness and sometimes with hostility. He was even publicly insulted at Mantua by the German, Gregory van Heimburg. The king of France, to whom he gave for the first time the title of Most Christian, did not prove any more willing than the others and brandished the threat of his Pragmatic Sanction, the charter of what was later to become Gallicanism. Pius II left Mantua on January 19th, 1460. The projected Crusade was to remain a mere paper scheme. Shortly after he left the city, he published the famous Bull *Execrabilis* which excommunicated all who appealed from the pope to the Council. During the next few years, he was constantly struggling against troubles in Rome, the claimants to the kingdom of Naples and the banditry of men like Piccinino and other more obscure *condottieri*, against tyrants such as Sigismund Malatesta at Rimini, a semi-pagan who even went so far as to poke fun at Christian rites and to fill, by night, a holy water stoup with ink so as to derive amusement from the figure the Christians cut as they came into the church. Pius II adopted very subtle tactics in his dealings with Louis XI who was then king of France. The point at issue was always the Pragmatic Sanction. In Germany, where Heimburg extended his influence to the full against the papacy, he received nothing but insults in spite of the efforts of his legate, Nicholas of Cusa. The latter died on August 11th, 1464. Shortly afterwards the pope, almost in despair at having failed to organize his Crusade, followed him to the grave.

At the outset of his pontificate, Pius II had set up a commission for the reform of the Curia. Cusa had worked out a scheme and suggested the establishment of three permanent "visitors" for the Church. Thas had been Nicholas V's intention. But none of the plans then formulated had been able to be implemented.

This pope has been blamed for showing excessive favour towards the Sienese. This attitude of his was a kind of attenuated nepotism. He was most anxious to canonize Catherine of Siena and he did so in 1461. One of the great joys of his life was to receive from Morea the head of St Andrew. He organized a magnificent reception ceremony for it in Rome in 1462. He made so many gifts to his native village of Corsignano that it became the town of Pienza. It has a celebrated cathedral. In the year before his death, when a pamphleteer taxed him with the more or less licentious writings of his youth, he answered him with admirable frankness and courage, while admitting and repudiating the errors of his past. In the course of this reply he wrote the phrase which has become famous: "Banish Aeneas, hold fast to Pius!"

As the Turks continued to advance, he travelled in person in the direction of Ancona with the intention of giving some impetus to the Crusade for so long delayed. He reached Ancona on July 19th, 1464. He died there on August 19th, just as the Venetian fleet at last joined forces with him. His death put an end to all desire for war against Islam.

PAUL II (1464–71)

After the death of Callistus III there had been a strong reaction against the Catalans in his household. On the death of Pius II, there was a somewhat similar reaction against the Sienese. The conclave which opened on August 30th, under the presidency of the great Cardinal Bessarion, chose as his successor Cardinal Barbo, a handsome, wealthy man, a nephew of Pope Eugenius IV and a native of Venice. He took the name of Paul II. He was forty-eight years old and had been a cardinal for twenty-four. He had distinguished himself as a collector of antique precious stones and coins. He was by nature gentle, peace-loving and generous. He had an impressive and majestic presence. He was criticized for his display, his vanity and a tendency to jealousy. The humanists, against whose demands he had to struggle from the beginning, wrongly blackened his memory by declaring that he was the enemy of literature and the arts. The truth of the matter is that the humanists were then becoming increasingly venomous; they proved themselves to be greedy, hypocritical and aggressive and to such a degree that they were becoming a danger to Christian faith. The most inveterate among them was Platina (Bartolomeo Sacchi, 1421–81). He was later to write a history of the popes, the first of its kind, and to revenge himself on Paul II by speaking very ill of him in its pages. Paul II, indignant at the opposition he encountered from this man when he made an attempt to reform the "College of Abbreviators" to which Platina belonged, had him imprisoned for a period of four months. This was the sort of treatment a humanist of that period and stamp could not forget. But present-day historians would be wrong to allow themselves to be misled by the insinuations of an enemy of a pope who, on the whole, was a clearsighted man. We may add that Platina, when in prison, toadied in a most abject manner so as to obtain his release. The neo-pagan, Pomponio Leto, was no less abject. He was the founder of a Roman Academy thoroughly imbued with an anti-Christian spirit. It was perfectly natural and legitimate for Pius II to take severe measures. Platina and Leto duly apologized but later it became clear that this was mere play-acting on their part.

In actual fact it was Paul II who introduced to Rome the new art of printing. Many editions of the great classics were printed there (Cicero, Lactantius, St Augustine, Donatus, as well as Livy, Aulus Gellius, Strabo, Pliny, etc.). Paul II was an enlightened patron of architects. It was he who built the Palazzo di Venezia. Nor did he lose sight of the Crusade. During his reign, the courageous Scanderbeg was welcomed at Rome in 1466. Albania was invaded by the Turks at the time. He obtained considerable subsidies. His citadel at Croja was relieved, but he himself died on January 17th, 1468.

Towards the kings and princes of Europe, Paul II adopted the same attitude as his predecessors. On the whole he was firm and exacting, but for the most part to no purpose. The efforts to reform the Curia remained in abeyance. Paul II endeavoured to choose good bishops for Italy and good cardinals for Rome. He received outstanding help from men like Bessarion and Carvajal. The latter was said to wear a hair-shirt under the purple. He had all his work cut out to counter the Czech, Podiebrad, whose treacherous counsellor was Heimburg. He was eventually excommunicated. Carvajal died on December 6th, 1469. Podiebrad died soon after in March 1471. Heimburg, now reconciled with the Church, passed away in August 1472.

A characteristic feature of the times is that the pope, in his own States, had to fight the banditry of the Anguillara whose chief, Everso, was the typical bandit baron. The whole band was tracked down. Sixteen castles bursting with their spoil were taken from them.

The question of the Crusade had been revived once more, but still to no purpose, when it was learned that the Turks had captured Negropont in Euboea, a Venetian possession. The pope again appealed to the Powers. Terror reigned in Italy. A league against the Turks was signed in Rome on December 22nd, 1470. The replies from the Christian princes were slow to come and the pope died rather suddenly of apoplexy on July 26th, 1471. Although Paul II was too addicted to extravagant luxury, it must be admitted that he was a devout, peaceful, just and beneficent pontiff. Even Platina's angry outbursts found nothing serious with which to reproach him. After him, things were unfortunately to take a turn for the worse.

SIXTUS IV (1471–84)

Yet the cardinals did not choose badly when, on August 9th, 1471, they elected Cardinal Francesco della Rovere, who took the name Sixtus IV.

He belonged to an old Ligurian family which had become impoverished. His mother, who had feared he might die, had consecrated him at an early age to St Francis. He was born in 1414 at Cella near Savona and, at the age of nine, had been entrusted to the Friars Minor. They had given him a fine education, encouraged him to study, made use of him as a teacher in their principal advanced schools at Padua, Bologna, Pavia, Siena, Florence and Perugia. He had been a success in all of them.

At the age of fifty, in 1464, he became minister-general of the Order and a cardinal three years later. Now at length, at the age of fifty-seven, he had become pope. He was a man of middle height, vigorous and broad, with a powerful and dominating head, or so it seemed. In fact, he proved

deplorably weak, above all in his dealings with his numerous
nephews and nieces whom he wished at all costs to enrich.
Paul II had left a considerable sum of money with the
Crusade in mind. Sixtus IV soon squandered it.

True, he did not abandon the idea of the Crusade. As his
predecessors had done, he promulgated a Bull against the
Turks and sent legates to the Powers to league them together
against the common enemy. Like previous pontiffs, he met
everywhere with moderate success or complete failure.

Meanwhile in Rome the pope allowed himself to be
monopolized by his nephews and nieces. He was incapable of
saying no to them. He had made Julian della Rovere a cardinal. There was something to be said for this since the young
man who was later to become the celebrated Pope Julius II
had talent. But the elevation to the purple of another nephew,
Peter Riario, was deplorable. He was a monstrous libertine.
His debaucheries killed him prematurely and he was replaced
in his uncle's favour by his brother, Jerome Riario, who was
almost as bad a character. Sixtus IV provided all his relatives
with enormous revenues by loading them with bishoprics and
lucrative abbeys. Under the instigation of the Riario brothers,
whom the pope allowed to do as they liked, Rome was the
scene of scandalous festivities, huge banquets, genuine orgies,
on the occasion of the weddings of the pontiff's nieces and
nephews or for visiting princes of the most disreputable sort,
such as Ferrante of Naples.

In 1745 Sixtus IV inaugurated a great Jubilee year. It was
on this occasion that he built the Ponte Sisto over the Tiber
and gave it his own name. Rome was cleaned up. The cardinals vied with the pope in preparing for a triumphant jubilee
year. The streets were cleaned and embellished. Pilgrims were
few at first but arrived in great numbers later and among
them were princes.

One of the most regrettable incidents during this pontificate
was the "Pazzi conspiracy" against the Medici who ruled
Florence. During Mass in the cathedral, Julian de' Medici

was assassinated and his brother Lorenzo only just escaped
the murderers' daggers. But the conspiracy eventually failed
and Lorenzo took a bitter revenge. Archbishop Salviati and
the principal conspirators were hanged. The most deplorable
feature of the whole affair is that it transpired that the pope's
nephews had been involved in the plot. The pope had been
told of everything and had limited himself to recommending
on several occasions that "on no account should any blood
be shed".

There was a strong reaction at Florence in favour of the
Medici. The pope had to threaten to place the city under an
interdict in order to prevent executions. Eventually Lorenzo
reluctantly submitted, but the prestige of the papacy did not
emerge unscathed after so scandalous a drama.

All this did little to stop the advance of the Turks. In 1480
the siege of Rhodes threw Christendom into dismay. De-
liverance came both through the heroic defence of the knights
under their grand master, Pierre d'Aubusson, and above all
because Mohammed II died in 1481. This was to lead to a
struggle for the succession between his sons, Bajazet II and
Djem. The latter in fact, who escaped with difficulty from
Byzantium, came to take refuge in Rome. He was to be used
as a hostage and a bulwark against Islam for a period of ten
years. The city of Otranto which had been captured, to the
great terror of the Neapolitans, was retaken on September 10th, 1481.

Until the end of his life, the pope had to contend with
conflicts between princes and republics in Italy. Like many of
his predecessors, he died of gout (August 12th, 1484). His
nephew Julian della Rovere built him a sumptuous tomb,
entrusted to the hands of the Florentine master, Antonio
Pollajuolo. It was in the "Renaissance" style, that is, completely covered with semi-pagan emblems and half-naked
figures. We cannot take leave of this pontiff without reminding
the reader that the Sistine Chapel in the Vatican bears his
name, since he began its construction. It was only completed

in the pontificate of his nephew, Julius II, and by Michelangelo.

INNOCENT VIII (1484–92)

On the death of Sixtus IV, Rome was pestered by the intrigues of his nephew, Jerome Riario, who had to be bribed before he would surrender the Sant' Angelo Castle. The conclave opened on August 25th. Twenty-five cardinals were present, twenty-one of them Italians. As at previous elections and in spite of the illusory character of the process, the cardinals attempted to impose conditions—*capitulations*, as they were then called—on the future pope. The government of the Church should become, so they said, collegial instead of remaining monarchical. Further, Cardinal Rodrigo Borgia, who thought his time had come, did all he could to have himself elected and did not hesitate to make simoniacal promises.

However he was not elected. On August 29th, Cardinal Cibo, after a sorry process of bargaining, was the winner and took the name of Innocent VIII. This title scarcely tallied with his past. He was fifty-two years old, of medium height, with a very pale face and expressionless eyes. He belonged to a patrician Genoese family which explains the favour he soon showed towards his fellow-countryman, Julian della Rovere. Before he had become a priest, he had had two children, both illegitimate. After his ordination, he had led a regular life. He was gentle and affable but his weakness of character was beyond belief and his forbearance beyond all legitimate bounds. The openly expressed aims of his policy were excellent: peace between princes, justice and the good of the State. If these aims were to be pursued effectively it was essential to have a less hesitant, less feeble, less ailing pontiff. Rivalries between princes, political assassinations, disturbances of all kinds continued to increase. If the Turkish peril had become less pressing it was still far from having disappeared and appeals for the Crusade were as useless as ever.

The pope gave little in the way of energetic example but the state of the Sacred College in his time was still more alarming. The Court of Rome was undoubtedly on the downgrade from the moral point of view. Some of the cardinals lived most worldly lives of luxury and immoral conduct. Although they were protectors of the arts and literature, they behaved like Renaissance princes. They may not have sunk so low as they into vice and immorality but they were not fundamentally different from the rest. The most deplorable cases were those of Rodrigo Borgia, the future Alexander VI, the most scandalous of them all, although one of the most intelligent and skilful in public affairs; Ascagno Sforza, his rival in every field, immorality included; Federico Sanseverino, who was little better, and Battista Orsini. From February 1485, these were joined by the wretched French cardinal La Balue who had been both the favourite and then the victim of Louis XI. Julian della Rovere must be placed at a much higher level. He was ambitious, violent, worldly, but never base or petty. He had three illegitimate daughters and suffered from what was then called "the French disease".

Voices were raised in the Church to prophesy retribution and catastrophe. Among these prophets we must number at once the extraordinary monk, Girolamo Savonarola. In the same year in which Pope Innocent VIII died, he had a dream which he considered a divine revelation. A hand appeared to him bearing a naked sword and he heard the words: "Soon the sword of the Lord will fall upon the earth." At the same time he heard other words promising divine mercy to the good and punishment for evil men.

Innocent VIII's death was more edifying than his life. From his sick-bed, he made a speech to the cardinals asking pardon for his failure to show himself equal to his task and exhorting them to choose a better pope to succeed him. He then received the sacrament of Extreme Unction and died, after an agony which lasted for five days, during the night of July 25th to the 26th. It was just one week before another

Genoese, Christopher Columbus, set out from the port of Palos to discover the New World.

Innocent VIII longed for a better pope to succeed him. His wish, touching though it was, was not fulfilled. But it was he who, by his choice of cardinals (among whom was a boy of fourteen, Giovanni Medici, the future Leo X) had prepared the way for the worst choice ever made in the history of the papacy. The hour of Rodrigo Borgia, for which he had so long waited, was about to come.

CHAPTER II

THE PAPACY FROM 1492

TO 1521

ALEXANDER VI (1492–1503)

It is not without a sense of shame that we come to the story of Alexander VI. We would do well to remember the words of Leo XIII: "The Church has no need of our lies." We must tell the truth as it happened and hide nothing. Newman compared the Church in those days to Christ borne bodily away by Satan. Pope Paul IV rightly said sixty years later that, if the Church were not immortal and divine, her representatives would have destroyed her at this period.

The cardinals would have made an excellent choice had they elected their colleague, Ardicino della Porta. But Rodrigo Borgia was firmly resolved not to let this election pass without gaining the tiara for himself. He had been the vice-chancellor and possessed great benefices with which he could buy votes. It was said that he had no less than sixteen bishoprics in Spain and rich abbeys in various places. He succeeded in gaining the support of Ascagno Sforza. He must have paid a high price for this. The conclave opened on August 6th, 1492. Twenty-three cardinals were present and on the morning of the 11th they elected the man for whom none of them could have had any respect. The election was undoubtedly simoniacal and so gravely illegal, yet it was probably valid according to the law then in force. It was only a little later that Julian della Rovere as Pope Julius II published a Constitution declaring null and void an election tainted with simony.

However severe we have to be towards this unworthy pontiff, surrounded by the illegitimate children of several mistresses, we must not pass over the very great human qualities he possessed. Although he was a Renaissance prince rather than a pope, he was an active and energetic prince. Historians rightly praise his experience of men and affairs, his diplomatic and political skill. A contemporary said of him: "He was a most intelligent man, hardworking and liberal, and his election was popular since it brought honour and reputation to the Roman Church." Even Luther hurls fewer anathemas at this sensual man than at Julius II whom we rank far above him but who behaved too often like a military commander instead of a man of God. Alexander VI was sixty years old. Advancing age had not extinguished his passions, but he had a majestic appearance in spite of his thick lips, his strong snub nose and his bald head. He received congratulations from various places. His election did not cause the scandal we might think. The times were so feverish, sensual, violent and disturbed. R. Garnett in *The Cambridge Modern History* has written of him: "Personally, indeed, he was never popular, but his efficiency as an administrator formed the brightest side of his character and his care for the material interests of his subjects was exemplary. Years afterwards, those who had most detested the man wished back the ruler for his 'good government and the plenty of all things in his time'."

He began well. Before him there had been no less than 220 murders in the course of a month. He re-established public order and security with great firmness. Finances were administered with prudence. His household was well behaved and kept in order. But his paternal weakness very soon became increasingly evident. His host of children, each out to feather his own nest, was the principal calamity of his reign. He had a favourite, Lucrezia Borgia, and this gave rise to the most atrocious calumnies and provided later centuries with a theme based on the falsest of presuppositions. In fact, Lucrezia was one of the chief victims of her father's policy, and her last years showed that she had a profound faith and was even devout.

The pope's evil genius was not his daughter but his son, Cesare Borgia, whom he quickly made archbishop of Valencia and then a cardinal although he really cared for nothing but war and adventure. In Machiavelli's view, he was the perfect model of the "Prince" as the opinion of the time conceived him. That is, he was the type of the ambitious man, without scruples, who did everything in the interests of his own advancement and stopped at nothing to gain his own ends. He soon threw the cardinal's purple aside and lived his own life as a *condottiere*. Every day passed in cunning and the exercise of force. We should not be surprised. This was the law of the times. A man like Cesare Borgia was at home in the century of the Malatesta, the Sforza, the Baglione, the Ferrante of Naples and a host of others less well known. He sums up a whole world in his person. It was to need all the eminent sanctity of a Francis Borgia, the third general of the Jesuits, to counterbalance the crimes of the family.

Among these crimes was one which so terrified and distressed the pope himself that he publicly confessed his sins and promised to mend his ways. And he gave the whole Curia an urgent invitation to imitate him in this act of penitence. The crime in question was the following: one morning in 1497 the pope had been informed that the body of his eldest son, John, duke of Gandia, had been dragged from the Tiber. Who had murdered him? The only witness that could be found, a wood merchant who lived near the river, stated that he had seen a dead body thrown into the water but that this was so usual that he had not thought it necessary to pass on the information to the police. Lucrezia's husband, John Sforza, was suspected and, with more likelihood, the sinister Cesare Borgia, standard-bearer of the Church.

Alexander VI appeared determined to keep his word. A Bull was planned and composed for the reform of the cardinals, the proper regulation of papal taxation and the correction of the most flagrant abuses in Christendom. But the Bull was never issued. The pope returned to his evil ways, the cardinals breathed a sigh of relief, the curial officials continued their petty intrigues, and disorder still flaunted itself in the Church. Yet one passionate, powerful, avenging voice was raised to save the honour of the Christian people at this sad moment in its history.

SAVONAROLA

During the century there had been very great and very successful preachers. Apart from the astounding Vincent Ferrer, who died in 1419, we may mention Bernardine of Siena (died 1444), John Capistran (died 1456), James of the March (died 1479). Savonarola belongs to this same line but had special characteristics of his own, his preaching was far more poignant and his end more tragic.

Girolamo Savonarola was born at Ferrara on September 21st, 1452. As the result of a sermon preached by an Augustinian friar, and without the knowledge of his family, he joined the Dominican Order. Among his papers his parents found a piece of writing entitled "On despising the World". In this document, the impetuous adolescent was already denouncing the abominable abuses of his times. He could see nothing good around him and yet we are quite certain that good elements were not entirely absent. It is clear then that he took a completely pessimistic view. During the first year of his life in religion he wrote a poem "On the decadence of the Church". As a young monk he consoled himself by prayer and ascetic practices. In 1481 or 1483 his superiors sent him to Florence. His early preaching was undistinguished. Another Dominican, Fra Mariano, was considered far more eloquent. But from 1484–5 onward,

Savonarola, who was then preaching at San Gimignano, began to pose as a prophet. And for his contemporaries it was from this period that he became a prophet of doom. He foretold retribution and he saw it as imminent. People listened to him and admired him. He took heart although his lack of success at Florence had discouraged him. In a letter to his mother, written during January 1489, he declared himself ready to devote "soul and body and all the knowledge God has given me to the service of divine love and the salvation of my neighbour". At Brescia, in 1486, he had taken the Apocalypse as the subject of his sermons. We may easily guess all that he was able to elicit from the burning pages of this book. He returned to it in 1490 but this time at the Dominican house of San Marco, so beautifully adorned by the paintings of Fra Angelico. He immediately became famous. Crowds thronged to hear him. The Dominican church was too small. They wanted him to preach in 1491 at the Duomo. It was at this time that Savonarola reached the height of his powers as an orator.

In the pulpit this friar, whose appearance in ordinary life was quite average, became another man. The little Dominican with his pale face, his wrinkled forehead, his aquiline nose, seemed full of fire and flame. He preferred to take as the subject of his long and powerful sermons one or other of the ancient prophets, and he then seemed himself to be transformed into one of them. He invented a new way of preaching. There were no flowery passages, no attempts at high-flown oratory. He made continual reference to Scripture. He re-echoed ceaselessly the Church's outcry against the prevalent corruption by inveighing time and again without compromise or pity against luxury, immorality and earthly vanities. As the stenographers took down his burning words their tears fell unrestrainedly on to the paper.

Lorenzo de' Medici very soon became disturbed by the ascendancy of this monk over the city which was under his own authority. He tried to win him over or at least to persuade him to be more moderate, but all to no purpose. In 1493, the pope agrèed to separate the Tuscan and Lombard Provinces of the Dominican Order. This made Girolamo more independent. Acting with a vigour which none could resist, he reformed his monastery of San Marco. He himself set the example of a more holy and mortified life. Vocations came by the dozen. In 1494, events led him—unfortunately—to mix high politics with religion in his sermons.

At that time the king of France, Charles VIII, a poor creature with a sick, fevered brain, was marching through Italy on his way to take possession of the kingdom of Naples and to prepare for the reconquest of Constantinople. Savonarola, on this occasion a false prophet, looked on him as the instrument of God's vengeance. He spoke of the coming of the French as a new "Flood". The Florentines lived through a time of terror. The Medici were expelled from the city. During the French occupation Savonarola alone was able to maintain order and good behaviour. He became the city's master. He immediately thought that he would make Florence the capital of Christian reform. It would be the city of Jesus Christ. From Florence the reign of God would spread throughout Italy and from Italy to the whole of Europe. And he, Savonarola, would be the interpreter of God's will. The friars who lived with him became infected with his fervour. Fra Silvestro Maruffi, who was a sleep-walker, had visions which upheld Brother Girolamo's plans. He now began to thunder against pagan humanism, against the pagan Renaissance, against the indecent canvases of the painters, against the introduction of pagan figures and allusions into the very churches themselves. Before him, John Capistran had practised what was now to be called "the burning of the vanities". Savonarola, in his turn, asked for a bonfire to be made of all luxury articles, all pictures in which liberties had been taken, all suggestive paintings and statues in the nude and all the instruments of sin. He won over the children and by using them struck terror into private homes. They went into them and hunted for all the ornaments and jewels their preacher had denounced as pagan. Florence was delivered over to a veritable puritan rule of terror. "The burning of the vanities" became an edifying spectacle and a kind of theatrical performance. Savonarola was overjoyed. He now began to utter purely political prophecies and opposed the return of the Medici. But all this could not fail in the end to weary some and rouse increasing resistance from others. In fact, Florence became divided into two camps, the *Arrabbiati* or the "Enraged" who were against Savonarola and the *Piagnoni* or "Weepers" who were on his side.

SAVONAROLA AND ALEXANDER VI

From Rome the pope could not fail to follow very closely all that was going on in Florence. Astute man that he was, as a sinner even and well aware of it, he passed over the attacks on moral disorders, the inveighing against the Roman Curia, the calls for reform. In his heart of hearts, he admitted that the preacher was right up to a point. He considered that is was dangerous for this friar, zealous indeed but with no experience of the world, to meddle with politics. He was angry with him for having almost canonized the insolent advance of Charles VIII through Italy. He himself manœuvred so skilfully against the French that Italian public opinion was grateful to him for his prudence and coolheadedness. Charles VIII was received in Rome but the pope did not yield on any point and the king of France eventually came to an agreement with him. After the French had gone and after the famous day of Fornovo, where both sides claimed the victory but which put an end to the nightmare of Charles VIII's armies, the pope judged the moment had come to intervene. He did so but showed moderation and prudence. On July 21st, 1495, he wrote a very friendly brief inviting Savonarola to come to Rome and explain his position. On July 31st, the friar replied that he acknowledged his duty to obey the pope but stated that he was in poor health. On September 8th a new brief came from the pope. This time it was addressed to the community of Santa Croce which was known to be hostile to the Dominicans. Mention was made in it of "a certain Savonarola" who claimed to be a prophet without providing proof of his worth and his mandate in the shape of miracles. The pope forbade him to preach. Savonarola appeared to be willing to submit but he then sent a letter to the pope on September 29th. It was couched in evasive and vague terms. The pope confined himself to renewing his order that Savonarola was not to preach. But pressure was now brought to bear on the pope who was asked to withdraw his prohibition, and on Savonarola who was told to take no notice of it. On February 11th, 1496, the friar in fact decided to resume his sermons. He justified his decision on the grounds that he had doubts as to whether the pope's prohibition was in accordance with God's will. Gradually he returned to the most passionate denunciations of his early sermons against the corruption of the Church. We need only quote the following typical extract, taken from Daniel-Rops' book *Eglise de la Renaissance et de la Réforme*:

> Stand forth, oh Church of infamy! Listen to what our Lord says to you: "I have clothed you in fine garments, but you have clothed idols with them. I have given you precious vessels but you have used them to inflame your pride. You have profaned my sacraments by your simony. Your lechery has made you a prostitute and taken away your beauty. And you do not even blush for your sins. Harlot that you are! She sits on the throne of Solomon, she beckons to all who pass by. Those with money go into her house and do what they will with her, but those who desire what is good are cast out."

These words were spoken in the Duomo at Florence during Lent in 1497. It is not difficult to understand that such expressions raised a storm of emotions. The pope saw that he must take severe measures. At Florence itself, opposition was growing stronger. Scuffles sometimes occurred round the pulpit of the self-appointed dictator. On May 13th, 1497, the pope signed a brief of excommunication. But Savonarola wrote a protest on June 19th against this condemnation which he declared "invalid before God and men". The struggle between the pope and the friar continued for another year. Florence wanted to save its "prophet" but the pope wanted to be obeyed and he threatened to place the city under an interdict, and to such good effect that the Signoria itself forbade Savonarola to preach. The latter, on March 13th, 1498, was imprudent enough to appeal to the Council against a "simoniacal, heretical and unbelieving pope". When they saw him in revolt against the censures passed on him, a number of his friends ceased to support his cause. It was at this time that a Franciscan as fanatical as himself offered to go publicly to the stake provided Savonarola did the same.

He refused and his popularity immediately collapsed. One of his brethren offered to take his place but to no purpose. On April 8th, 1498, Savonarola was arrested and imprisoned. He was brought to trial and put to the torture. The pain he endured caused him to admit that his prophecies were all false. His brethren abandoned him with the exception of two who were condemned to the stake with him on May 22nd, and executed on the 23rd.

Such is the amazing story of this extraordinary man who has been the subject of discussion ever since. The Protestants claimed that he was one of Luther's forerunners. It cannot be doubted that this is a gross error. We would say that he was an ascetic, an apostle, thoroughly imbued with a sense of the eternal and the divine, and in revolt against the neo-paganism of his century. He was right, absolutely right, as far as fundamental issues were concerned, but he was carried away by his imagination and zeal beyond all reasonable bounds. St Bridget and St Catherine of Siena had thundered out their protests just as he had done. Great minds, saints even, have held his memory in veneration. And he deserved that they should, for he was sincere and loved our Lord

Jesus Christ. Among those who venerated him were Michel-angelo, St Catherine de Ricci, St Philip Neri and others. His tragedy was the tragedy of a whole century, just as Luther's was soon to be, though in a sense more disastrous for Christendom.

It is sad to have to add that after his death, Alexander VI continued, as though nothing had happened, to scandalize the Church both by his own behaviour and by that of his in-famous son, Cesare Borgia. All came to an end with the death of the pope from pernicious malaria on August 18th, 1503, and the complete destruction of the insolent wealth of the Borgias. To the credit of this lamentable pope let it be noted that he succeeded in establishing between the Portuguese and the Spanish, rivals in their discoveries, a useful line of de-marcation running 100 Spanish leagues west of the Azores (May 4th, 1493). The distance was increased to 270 leagues by the Treaty of Tordesillas (June 7th, 1494). Finally, the pope did not fail to celebrate (and successfully) the Jubilee in the year 1500.

The fact remains that he considerably lowered the prestige of the papacy. It was not to be restored to any appreciable extent under his immediate successors whose pontificates we shall now rapidly summarize.

JULIUS II (1503–13)

After the unworthy Alexander VI, the cardinals elected an excellent pope, Cardinal Francesco Piccolomini, a nephew of Pius II, a worthy and virtuous man. He took the name of Pius III. But he only reigned for twenty-six days from Sep-tember 22nd to October 18th, 1503. The cardinals were fully conscious of the need for the Church to have an energetic and fighting pontiff and they elected as his successor Julian della Rovere after one of the shortest conclaves ever held (October 31st, 1503). He was the strongest personality in the Church and the period. He was admired but perhaps feared rather than loved. In summing up his character historians have used the words terrible, huge, gigantic, titanesque. He was imperious, violent yet always noble. His speech was rough, earthy, picturesque.

His ambition was to restore to the papacy its political authority and this led him to be more of a warrior than a priest. A famous saying of his has come down to us: *Fuori i barbari!* ("Out with the barbarians!") Among these "barbarians" was the king of France, Louis XII, against whom he formed the Holy League in 1511. While the pope threatened the French with his material weapons, Louis XII conceived the idea of using spiritual arms against him in return. With the help of a few discontented cardinals, he called a Council at Pisa. The date for its opening was September 1st, 1511. Julius II was not the man to take this insult lying down. He reacted with his usual vigour and, on July 18th, 1511 in the Bull *Sacrosanctae romanae Ecclesiae*, he himself convened a Council at the Lateran to open on April 19th, 1512. It was to be an Ecumenical Council, the eighteenth in the Church's history. Only French prelates came to Pisa, two archbishops and fourteen bishops, representatives of the French universities and large numbers of theologians and canonists. Cardinal Carvajal the younger presided. This bogus council opened on November 5th, 1511, but the hostile attitude of the people of the city forced it very soon to take refuge, though without changing its name, at Milan and later at Asti, Turin and finally Lyons where it died a natural death and left no traces. Julius II had of course deposed the rebellious cardinals, on October 24th, 1511, and subsequently he placed the whole kingdom of France under an interdict, with the exception of Brittany.

THE LATERAN COUNCIL

The fifth Council of the Lateran itself opened on May 10th, 1512. It was attended by fifteen cardinals and seventy-nine bishops, most of whom were Italians. Their number eventually increased to 120. The opening speech, and it was a very remarkable one, was made by Giles of Viterbo (Egidio Canisio), the general of the Augustinians. With striking frankness, he spoke of the need to reform the Church. The pope, he said, had achieved great success by force of arms. But this is not the way the Church likes to act. Her arms are, above all, devotion, prayer and a lively, sincere faith. It was with arms such as these that she would conquer her enemies, both those from within and those from without. One memorable phrase in his speech stands out: *We may change men by means of what is holy, we may not change what is holy by means of men.*

Sessions two to four, from May 17th, 1512, to February 16th, 1513, were held during the pontificate of Julius II. Their aim was to declare the illegality of the Council of Pisa-Milan and then, in collaboration with the pope, to place France under an interdict. On December 3rd, 1512, an envoy of the Emperor Maximilian, who had hitherto supported the king of France, Louis XII, arrived and stated that his master had rallied to the side of the pope and the Lateran Council. On December 10th, 1512, the "Pragmatic Sanction" of Bourges was condemned. This was the charter of Gallicanism and was constantly used by France as a threat against the Holy See.

On February 21st, Pope Julius II died. On his deathbed he declared that, as Julian della Rovere, he forgave the rebellious cardinals, but that, as pope, he condemned them. This pontiff who had been the subject of so much discussion was a man of intense faith. His last wishes were expressed with strength and wisdom. He left large sums of money to poor priests, asking them to pray for his soul. On February 20th he received Holy Communion with admirable devotion. To his astonished household, this "terrible" pope had all the appearances of a saint.

Julius II was the object of a severe judgement by his contemporary, Guicciardini, and by a scholar of the first rank, Gregorovius. The truth of the matter is that his piety was sincere but too intermittent. He thought seriously of reforming the Church. Although he had too great a liking for war, he was convinced that he was preserving the independence of the Holy See in a perilous century, by obtaining for it undisputable political authority. It is in this sense that Burckhardt, the historian of the Renaissance, called him "the saviour of the papacy". Friends of the arts also extol in him an intelligent and generous patron. It is pleasant to recall his relations, sometimes stormy but always on a very high level, with a man like Michelangelo; the favour he showed towards Raphael; the magnificent plans he had in mind for the honour of the Church in the sense in which it had been understood by Nicholas V with his policy of "magnificence". Julius II was not a learned man but he loved learning. Through his efforts Rome became, to a somewhat greater extent, the capital of enlightenment. The sixteenth century has been called "the century of Leo X". It would be equally, if not more, correct to call it the century of Julius II. In our own days it is not this type of pope we venerate and desire. But in his own time, Julius was a great pontiff and perhaps the man the situation required.

LEO X (1513–21)

It is an almost incredible yet certain fact that when Julius II's death seemed imminent, the Emperor Maximilian, whose wife had died shortly before, offered himself as a candidate for the tiara. He did so in a letter to his sister Marguerite, regent of the Low Countries. He tried to secure his own nomination as the pope's coadjutor with right of succession. The letter was dated September 18th, 1511. Other documents guarantee its authenticity. It goes without saying that at the conclave after Julius II's death, no one gave a thought to the emperor, except perhaps to note that his childish ambition was a token of his recognition of the majesty of the papacy. On March 11th, 1513, Cardinal Giovanni Medici, son of

Lorenzo the Magnificent, was elected and took the name of Leo X.

The fact that he was a Medici promised well for the future. He would certainly be, like the rest of his family, a patron of the arts. His gentle character, goodness, virtue, above all his generosity, were highly praised. He was only thirty-eight and he had been a cardinal for twenty-four years. There was general rejoicing in the Church, especially at Florence where he was born on December 11th, 1475. He had been given tutors of great fame: Angiolo Politian, Bernardo Bibbiena, Marsilio Ficino. The last named attempted to combine the worship of Plato with that of Christ. The young man had hitherto lived a worldly but regular life. At the time of his election as pope he was still only a deacon. He was ordained priest on March 15th, consecrated a bishop and crowned on the 19th. His enthronement took place on April 11th, the feast of St Leo the Great. At the time a saying went the rounds. It summed up the two previous pontificates while at the same time made it clear what was expected of Leo's: "After Venus and Mars, Minerva is now on the throne."

THE CONTINUATION OF THE COUNCIL

One of Leo X's first acts was to order the reopening of the Council. Session six in fact took place on April 25th, 1513. Three commissions were set up, one to work for the establishment of peace between Christian princes, the second for the reform of the Church, the third for the preservation of the faith and extinction of the French schism. The latter was obtained by the submission of Louis XII on October 26th, 1513. The rebel cardinals, Carvajal the younger and Sanseverino, had already submitted and been granted full absolution.

On the same day, October 26th, the reform commission was divided into five sub-committees. But they did little more than reform the system of curial taxes which had been an object of complaint in the Church over a long period. The Bull *Pastoralis officii* (December 13th, 1513) dealt with this question. There was a solemn celebration during session eight on December 19th, to commemorate the reconciliation of the king of France with the Holy See.

Shortly afterwards the news came that Louis XII had died and had been succeeded by Francis I. There was much apprehension in Rome when it was learned that he had entered Italy at the head of a powerful army with the intention of conquering the duchy of Milan. Fear changed to terror at the news of the brilliant victory of the French at Marignano on September 13th and 14th, 1515. The attitude of the Italian courts changed perceptibly. The pope decided at once to come to terms with the conqueror. Francis I, for his part, was anxious for peace with the pope. The military successes of the French only accentuated these various tendencies. The king of France wanted to meet the pope. Bologna was chosen for the purpose. The pope, who was received with wild enthusiasm at Florence, had an icy welcome at Bologna which he reached on December 8th, 1815. On the other hand, Francis I was the object of much admiration when he made his entry on the 11th. A private meeting between Leo X and the king lasted two hours. Conversations continued in complete secrecy on the 12th and 13th. The king took his leave on the 15th but the negotiations continued with a view to the signing of a Concordat between Rome and France. This Concordat, which was to remain in force until the French Revolution, was only concluded after difficult discussions on August 18th, 1516. It was approved by the Council in its session eleven on December 19th of the same year. This explains why it is known as the Concordat of 1516. Its essential provision gave the king the right of appointment in his own kingdom to all major benefices (bishoprics and abbeys) while the pope was to be responsible for canonical investiture.

During the same session the Bull *Pastor Aeternus* was promulgated. It condemned the Pragmatic Sanction of 1438 and contained the following definition of papal power: "Only the reigning Roman pontiff possesses authority over all Councils. He calls them together, transfers and dissolves them. This full right and power are revealed both by the witness of Scripture, the writings of the Fathers and the decrees of former Roman pontiffs, our predecessors, by the decrees of the holy canons and by the declarations of Councils themselves."

The twelfth and last session of the Council took place on March 16th, 1517. Previous decrees were confirmed and the tithes or Church taxes, prescribed for the purpose of the Crusade against the Turks, were made obligatory for a further period of three years.

In France, strong opposition arose against the Concordat and hence against the Ecumenical character of this Council. The *Parlement* even attempted to resist the king in the matter of the registration of the Concordat. In fact, the Council was accepted throughout the Church as Ecumenical. But the meagre reforming decrees it issued remained a dead letter. Less than eight months after its close the Protestant revolt broke out. It claimed that it was finally achieving the reform announced and desired for centuries but which had never been carried out. In fact, this reform was only given shape and force after still more terrible struggles and another Council, that of Trent (1545–63). And so the reign of Leo X continued. Its brilliance cannot be denied in the realm of the arts and of literature, but it had great weaknesses from the point of view of religion. An entirely new spirit was needed throughout Christendom. In the next chapter we shall describe the spirit of the times through which it had just lived and the men, some of whom were of great stature, in whom this spirit was incarnate and who, as far as posterity is concerned, are its most eminent and significant representatives.

CHAPTER III

THE MEN AND THE SPIRIT

OF THE PERIOD

THE ITALIAN RENAISSANCE

At the period in the history of the Church with which we are concerned the Italian Renaissance was in full swing. It had begun a century before and it reached its zenith, the heyday of its glory, in 1450. But what is meant by the word "Renaissance", and why do we speak of the "Italian Renaissance"?

The word "Renaissance" suggests the idea of an awakening after a period of great darkness. Calvin once said: *Post tenebras lux* ("Light after darkness"). But men had held this view for the previous 200 years. The writers and artists of the fifteenth century in particular considered this the characteristic of their own times by comparison with what was later to be called "the Middle Ages", a term of opprobrium suggesting a time of darkness coming between two eras of light. Even down to our own day there have been historians who have given this erroneous account of events. Yet it is easy to realize the purely conventional and inaccurate character of this view of history. From the standpoint of art, we may well ask whether the Renaissance produced any works equal to our superb cathedrals. From the intellectual point of view, what men can it place above Thomas Aquinas, even Duns Scotus, and finally Dante Alighieri, who most certainly belongs to the "Middle Ages"? To say with Michelet that the Renaissance was the *awakening of reason* in opposition to *authoritarian dogma*, is surely to be inaccurate and tendentious.

The facts themselves must be closely examined. In the first place, we have used the expression "the Italian Renaissance". The historical phenomenon of the Renaissance did in fact make its appearance on Italian soil a century earlier than elsewhere and it attained there a brilliance which was unsurpassed. The reason lies in the fact that, during the long conflict between the papacy and the empire, a vigorous communal movement had sprung up in the country. Small republics came into existence in many places. They were full of activity, rich, original, boisterous. We need only mention Florence, Venice, Siena, Pisa and Genoa. These were flourishing cities, full of exuberant life. This alone would explain all the rest. They had their men of action, for whom the hitherto unknown word "genius" was coined. They remind us of the ancient cities of Greece in which, almost 2,000 years before, all the arts had reached such amazing perfection.

The turbulence of the Middle Ages did not die out with the progress of wealth and culture. On the contrary it grew more impassioned and expressed itself in fierce rivalry between the different parties, relentless struggles, savage vendettas and disordered ambitions. The day came almost everywhere when, among the ruins of communal freedom, there arose powerful tyrants, the product of audacity, pride and wealth. Milan was in the hands of the Visconti and then the Sforza; Florence in those of the Medici; Rimini in those of the Malatesta; Perugia in those of the Baglioni, etc. Military contractors known as *condottieri* hired mercenaries and sold their own services to the highest bidder and so made and destroyed whole fortunes. Side by side with this political evolution, a literary movement, influenced by it and often imitating its methods, also developed. It soon acquired the name of *humanism* and it became one of the essential ele-

ments of the Renaissance. In fact from the very beginning
an alliance was concluded between the powerful of this world
and the new intellectuals. The "tyrants" produced by the
political evolution needed the incense of praise and glory.
They became the patrons of the men of letters and the artists.
The former lauded their exploits while the latter embellished
their palaces. The *literati* or humanists were very willing to
collaborate in this way. They needed money, prebends and
patrons. *Humanism*, as we shall shortly define it, became a
lucrative and honoured career. Just as the princes or the
Republics bought the services of a *condottiere of the sword*,
so too they purchased those of a *condottiere of the pen*. Fame
was dispensed by writers. History as written by them was a
most valuable source of diplomatic power. Their writings
were the newspapers of the period. They made and unmade
public opinion. A skilful Latinist needed to set no limit to
his ambitions. He became the prince's confidential agent, his
factotum. Later he would be his counsellor, his ambassador,
his public orator. Full of pride in his own talents, the humanist,
greedy, in most cases at least, for wealth and pleasure, grew
intoxicated with the delights to which the prince's favour
admitted him. All his Christian feeling gradually died out
while at the same time familiarity with pagan authors instilled
in him the spirit of the paganism of antiquity. We are trying
here to discover what the spirit of the Renaissance actually
was. To a large extent it was neo-pagan.

HUMANISM

In classical Latin, Cicero's for example, the word *humanitas*
meant not only humanity or human nature but also intellectual culture, education, civilization, good breeding, elegance,
even the charm and delights of the spoken or written word.
In the fifteenth century, and even during the fourteenth in the
case of Dante and still more of Petrarch (1304–74) and
Boccaccio (1313–75), a reaction had set in against the distorted

Latin of the scholastics. While the politically ambitious were bursting the bonds of feudal organization, the humanists shattered the thought forms of the Middle Ages. Scholasticism had erected the great theological systems. Intent wholly on the construction of a strong and magnificent edifice, it had paid little attention to literary form. Everything had been sacrificed to clarity, sobriety and no allowance was made for stylistic ornament, for the charm of a well-turned phrase, in a word for *humanitas*. Hence humanism wished to return to classical antiquity. It had never ceased to be venerated but had long ceased to be understood. The humanists were men of letters, and a Ciceronian period, a verse of Horace, a canto of Virgil or a chapter of Livy sent them into ecstasies. From the time of Petrarch and Boccaccio, they also read Greek which had for long been almost unknown in the West. With the humanists there is a rebirth of the taste for form. The beauty, the rhythm and harmony of a sentence, the cadence of a line of poetry, are sought for their own sakes independently of their content. The doctrine of art for art's sake was already making its way into Christian circles which had hitherto strongly rejected it, sometimes even with considerable indignation. This was the major revolution of humanism. It is true that the most famous of the fourth and fifth century Fathers, men like Augustine, Jerome, Leo the Great, had sought and achieved stylistic elegance as it was understood in their own time. But for them form was only an accessory and subordinated to their thought. The humanists did not allow it to remain in this humble and secondary position. Form became supreme. The writings of the Middle Ages were judged solely from the point of view of their style and language. They were dismissed as "barbarian". Even Dante himself did not always escape their strictures since he had written in the vernacular. The Renaissance Latinists and Hellenists could not stomach anything written in a non-classical language. Petrarch's contemporaries had a far higher opinion of his Latin works than of the sonnets of his *Rime* written in the Italian of the period.

And just because they were philologists, the humanists were also archeologists. They threw themselves with delight upon old monastic libraries in which lay forgotten the manuscripts of the great writers of the past. Each discovery was an event. One of John XXII's secretaries, who accompanied his master to the Council of Constance, took advantage of the situation to pursue the chase in castles and monasteries, and he gloried in the discovery of a forgotten poem of Lucretius, or of some unknown work of Plautus, Cicero or Tacitus. The secretary's name was Poggio Bracciolini (1380–1459). Another, Thomas Parentucelli, who was to become pope under the name of Nicholas V, discovered the works of St Leo the Great. The fall of the Byzantine Empire a few years later drove the Greek scholars from their country and one of them, Cardinal Bessarion, brought with him 600 manuscripts which filled the humanists with joy. Once printing had become common, the books most often published were, in addition to the Bible, such classics as the works of Virgil, Caesar, Livy, Cicero and Sallust. Among the most erudite of the printers was the Venetian, Aldus Manutius (1449–1515), whose editions of the Greek authors remained until our own times the most perfect and the most distinguished in existence.

But this frequent and enthusiastic familiarity with the pagan authors was certainly not without its dangers for the Christian spirit in a century in which human passions were allowed free rein in the political sphere. It was scarcely possible for the humanists who served the potentates of the time (greedy as these were for power and pleasure) to be their secretaries and receive of their bounty, and at the same time preserve intact the faith of their childhood.

CHRISTIAN AND PAGAN HUMANISM

In actual fact, it is possible to distinguish two streams of humanism, the Christian and the pagan.

Among the outstanding Latinists who remained fundamentally Christian, we may mention Ambrogio Traversari, general of the Camaldolese, and his disciple, Gianozzo Manetti (1396–1459), the devout teacher, Vittorino da Feltre (1379–1447), Aeneas Sylvius Piccolomini, whose life we have sketched as Pius II (died 1464), etc.

But the pagan stream seems to include more names. Poggio Bracciolini whom we have already mentioned, earned his reputation chiefly from his scurrilous *Facetiae* which claimed to report conversations between members of the Pontifical Chancellery. They form a collection of piquant but too often disgraceful anecdotes.

The king among the humanists, Lorenzo Valla (1405–57), a papal secretary and a canon of the Lateran (where he is buried) was not only the author of *Six Books on the Elegancies of the Latin Tongue* (1444) and a refutation of the *Donation of Constantine*, but also of a very doubtful dialogue "On Pleasure and True Good" in which an open profession of Epicureanism does not fit at all well with that of the Christian faith. It is true that another famous humanist, Filelfo (1389–1481) also shows a strange sympathy for Epicurus, but he does so by offering him as an example of a peaceful, quiet life, wholly characterized by *alipia*, that is, by the absence of pain. When we remember that Christianity is humility, purity, charity, sacrifice, while paganism is pride, pleasure, derision, a love of the easy and undisciplined life, it is not easy to find examples of Christian living among the circle of the Epicureans. Another peculiarity which we find unpleasant is the ferocious jealousy which often set one humanist against another. Men like Poggio, Valla and Filelfo exchange insolent remarks which are only the prelude to the violent language which will soon be characteristic of Luther in his attacks on Rome and the "papists". It is to Valla that Erasmus is indebted for the wealth of sarcasm which fills his *Praise of Folly* (1509), for Valla was his ideal of the humanist. He reproduced his *Latin Elegancies* in his own *Colloquia* (1522). It is this critical spirit which inspired all his works.

To return to the Italian humanists, among the most dubious we must rank Antonio Beccadelli, known as Panormitanus (1394–1471), whose best known work is modelled on Catullus, Propertius and Ovid. He descended to the most vile obscenities and yet this did not prevent another great humanist of the period, Guarino of Verona, from writing a very laudatory preface to the book.

We have already pointed out the measures taken by Pope Paul II against such humanists as Platina and Pomponio Leto. And we must not forget the very great names of Marsilio Ficino and Pico della Mirandola, both polymaths.

When humanism crossed the Alps from Italy, its two streams were still in evidence, the earlier, profoundly Christian and devout humanism of a Rudolph Agricola (1442–85), an Alexander Hegius (died 1498), a Rudolph Lang (died 1519), a Jakob Wimpfeling (died 1528) and the neo-pagan humanism of Mutian and Hessus which was to produce such rebels as Crotus Rubianus and especially Ulrich von Hutten, who were the first to applaud the anti-Roman audacity of Luther. We feel inclined to put mid-way between the two Erasmus of Rotterdam, who in his turn became the king of the humanists. Yet he was to end his life as a Christian after he had earned the right to be called in our own day, the "Voltaire of the sixteenth century".

VIRTÙ

Since we are now attempting to identify the "spirit of the time", we are forced to say that there was a definite though gradual movement towards an increasingly non-Christian naturalism. The ideal of a man like Ignatius Loyola, the champion of Catholic reform, was to be *agere contra*: nature was to be resisted, mastered, made to submit to the law of the Gospel. The ideal of men like Valla, Poggio and Mutian and perhaps even of Erasmus, was rather *sequi naturam*.

In the sixteenth century, the man who propounded the doctrine which inspired the spirit of the time was Machiavelli

(1469–1527). More than any other this astute and sceptical Florentine had observed the men and especially the princes of the period. Long before Nietzsche, he understood that "man is an object who desires to be surpassed" or that he must at least realize all the possibilities he possesses. "You must become what you are." This advice seems like a moral precept but it goes beyond good and evil, beyond ordinary ethics. The ideal is summed up in a word it is almost impossible to translate: *virtù*. It would clearly be completely inaccurate to render it by *virtue.* It seems rather: *the will to dominate*, energy that is outside all moral control, the pride of being a *superman*, the resolve to live to the utmost limits of one's inherent powers, the passion of Lucifer crying out in exultation: *Quo non ascendam?* In a calm, cool tone, Machiavelli made all this clear in his political treatise *The Prince*. We are told he was inspired to write it by Cesare Borgia, the son of a pope, and one of the most astonishing phenomena of the century.

THE SAINTS

Over against these disturbing characters, these "heroes" of neo-pagan *virtù*, we may well ask whether the Church could set the kind of heroes she honours as saints and whom she declares to be so after a searching inquiry into their heroic virtues. Christendom is kept in being by its saints. We can be certain that the faith remained alive in the fifteenth century, that the deviations we have described only concerned imperceptible minorities. It would have been very astonishing if the Church had become too sterile to continue to give birth to saints. Although Bernardine of Siena died before 1450, he still had disciples six years later: John Capistran who died in 1456 and James of the March who died in 1476. The delightful Fra Angelico whom we consider an admirable artist was honoured in his time as a saint. He died in 1455. In the same year there died at Venice St Lawrence Justinian, the first patriarch of the city.

At Florence, which rivalled Rome as a centre of the arts and of letters, lived an eminent bishop, St Antoninus, a Dominican. He was to die in 1459. Nor must we forget Blessed Bernardine of Feltre (died 1494). He was a Franciscan, a popular missioner and the founder of pawnshops, institutions which the popes authorized and encouraged. There is Blessed Bernardine of Fossa (died 1503) who was also a Friar Minor; St Catherine of Bologna (died 1463), lady-in-waiting to Princess Marguerite of Este. She was a Franciscan tertiary and later became a Poor Clare (1432) and abbess of Bologna (1457). She was renowned for her prophecies, her miracles and her struggles with the devil. There was St Catherine of Genoa (died 1510) of the great house of Fieschi. She had married a man of loose morals. She converted him and after his death undertook to serve the sick. She showed her heroic courage during the plagues of 1497 and 1501. She too was favoured with exceptional graces and supernatural communications particularly regarding purgatory whose very existence Protestantism would shortly deny.

We end this summary list of great Christian souls who lived at this time with the name of St Francis of Paula. He was born of poor parents in Calabria in 1416. He had been given a home by the Franciscans but he left them when he was thirteen to lead the life of a hermit. His example was followed by others. A group of hermits grew up around him. He called them the Minimi (they were *the least* of all men), built a monastery and obtained the approval of Sixtus V. His reputation spread so widely that it reached the ears of the king of France, the "realist" Louis XI. Louis was so amazed by the recital of his virtues that he sent for him so that he might be helped on his death-bed by a genuine saint. Charles VIII held him in special esteem. Francis of Paula remained in France, a living reproach to the worldly and a model for those who longed for reform, bowed down as they were by the evils that afflicted the Church. He was to die at Plessis-lès-Tours on April 2nd, 1507, at the age of ninety-one. And the Church counted among her members many devout souls other than canonized saints, men like Thomas à Kempis to whom is ascribed the *Imitation of Christ*, a book which so many generations down to our own times have read and meditated upon. Thomas à Kempis died in 1471. Then there is Denis the Carthusian, a fervent follower of the great mystic Ruysbroeck. Denis, too, died in 1471; John Monbaer of the celebrated Congregation of Windesheim, a successful reformer, who died in France in the latter part of the year 1501; John Standonck (died 1504) another reformer who was attached to the Sorbonne from 1484 onward and whose ascetic life as master of the Montaigu College at Paris Erasmus so pitilessly derided.

The Sacred College itself, though dishonoured by worldly and ambitious cardinals, had among its members such very great figures as Capranica, Cesarini, Niccolo Albergati, Bessarion, Carvajal the elder, Nicholas of Cusa. The latter, who died in 1464, must not be seen only as a powerful and energetic reformer but also as one of the forerunners of modern science. And finally there was the French cardinal, Raimond Perauld. He was born at Surgères in the Saintes diocese in 1435 and died at Viterbo in 1505. The Holy See entrusted him on several occasions with missions of the greatest importance, particularly in connection with the furtherance of the Crusade. We have seen elsewhere what kind of man Girolamo Savonarola was, and although the Protestants have tried to annex him, somewhat rashly let it be said, this is all the more reason why we should rank him with those who brought honour to their times. On the morrow of the Protestant revolt, that is in November 1517, just as the fruitless Council of the Lateran was proving a failure, a man died in Spain who has been recently called by a French author "the model cardinal". Francisco Ximenes was not only unequalled as a statesman, he was also a great reformer of clerical and monastic morals, a friend to the ecclesiastical sciences, a promoter of the study of the Bible which Luther was to attempt to claim as his own preserve in order to use it against the Roman Church.

THE ARTS

We should have only an inadequate view of the vast movement which the Renaissance was if we saw in it nothing but popes, princes, humanists and the saints themselves. Before all else it was perhaps a prodigious flowering of the arts. Never at any time in history nor in any country in Europe or in the world have there been such remarkable artists as in Italy during the fifteenth and sixteenth centuries. Here we can only cast a quick glance at them. The arts at this period were closely united to religion. Public buildings were mostly churches (and castles); paintings had as their subjects the mysteries of the Christian faith, the Annunciation, the Adoration of the Magi, episodes from the Gospels, the Crucifixion, etc. But they also depicted the beauties of the earth, and there were portraits of famous persons. Sculpture was intended for the ornament of churches or the embellishment of tombs but also as a representation of the antique. Here again the spirit of the age is revealed as it is in the literature and the different types of great men. But whereas the names of the humanists are now only of academic interest to specialists, while the Latin works of which they were so proud are buried in the most profound oblivion, it must be said to the glory of the artists that they have bequeathed to posterity evidences of their genius which we may well call immortal. Just as our medieval cities are proud of their Gothic cathedrals, so too Italy proudly points to the achievements of great architects such as Brunelleschi (the Cathedral at Florence), Leone Battista Alberti (Santa Maria Novella in Florence), Bramante and Michelangelo (St Peter's at Rome). Then there are the sculptors Lorenzo Ghiberti, Donatello, Jacopo della Quercia, Antonio del Pollajuolo, Andrea del Verocchio, Luca della Robbia. Their art reaches its highest summit in Michelangelo Buonarotti.

Still more numerous are the painters whose pictures form the treasure of the museums of Italy and are to be found also in every European capital. The names of some of these men are household words: Masaccio, Fra Angelico, Filippo Lippi, Benozzo Gozzoli, Piero della Francesca, Cosimo Rosselli, Botticelli, Domenico Ghirlandajo, Filippino Lippi, Luca Signorelli, Melozzo da Forli, Pinturicchio, Perugino, Mantegna, Giovanni Bellini, Giorgione, all predecessors of Titian. And above all the rest, above all the great artists of all time, are the mighty, inimitable and unsurpassable three: Leonardo da Vinci, Raphael, Michelangelo.

But what is perhaps more extraordinary than all the rest is that many of the men we have just named, if not all of them, were artists of the type we might call "multi-valent" in that they excelled in everything. They were by turns architects, painters, sculptors, engineers, even writers and poets. This was the case with Leone Battista Alberti, Michelangelo, Raphael and above all with Leonardo da Vinci (died 1519). Never, we may say, has the human stock produced finer specimens and, on the whole, any that give greater honour to Christian civilization. If there is one thing which can help us to pass a less severe judgement on certain popes and great churchmen of the period, it is that they appreciated this new wonder and did their utmost to protect the men of letters and the artists of their time.

CONCLUSION

After this too cursory survey of the years between 1450 and 1517, the conclusion which is self-evident is that they were years of contrast and contradiction. The most reflective minds did not cease to think of the great event for which men had longed for centuries past. It was always a topic of conversation and yet it never happened or only appeared in timid outline or in partial achievements. This event was *the reform of the Church in its head and in its members.* Was Christianity to dissolve in an entirely human neo-paganism? Would Christ's promise to be with his Church until the end of time prove illusory? Would saints still come into the world? Would there be apostles full of zeal to preach the Gospel to the new worlds discovered by Christopher Columbus, Vasco da Gama, Magellan and so many other navigators of genius? Or would Christendom be divided into sections hostile one to another, sections that were frankly pagan and rationalist, sections that were half-pagan, sections inspired by an exacerbated and false mysticism, condemning all that is human and finding nothing of worth except in God alone? The world was waiting and the best souls were racked with suffering.

In our days, but for quite different reasons, we are undergoing the same kind of suffering. The events of the sixteenth century as they unfold may partly reassure us concerning the developments our children and grandchildren will experience. The Church does not die!

CHAPTER IV

THE PROTESTANT REVOLT

FROM 1517 TO 1534

THE CAUSES

Historians in general have not clearly understood the causes of the Protestant revolt. The majority of them imagine that the *abuses* which flaunted themselves in the Church produced a sudden upsurge of indignation in a few men with great influence over the masses. But these men themselves, Luther, Zwingli, Calvin did not see things in this light. If we understand them aright, it was not irregular conduct among monks, among bishops even and popes, which impelled them to revolt against Catholic tradition. If we are to believe them, it was rather essential *doctrinal deviations*, intolerable errors concerning the idea of original sin and redemption, salvation and grace, the relations of fallen man with God, the means of sanctification brought into the world by Jesus Christ, the place of human action in the divine plan for the renewal of the sinful soul cut off from its eternal destiny.

It was therefore a general *failure of faith* in the Church, a failure dating from quite a remote period, and concerned with her providential mission, which forced *men of faith* (they appropriated this title to themselves, refused it to others and founded all their teaching on faith alone) to protest against "man-made inventions" and to restore its primitive purity to Christ's revelation. After centuries of ignorance during which this shocking degradation of the divine message had been brought about, the "reformers", as they called themselves, tried to persuade the Christian world that they alone had received from the Holy Spirit the exalted mission of reviving and restoring the saving doctrine of Christ by purging it of all the dross of centuries.

From the outset, this view of things was openly put forward by Luther long before his revolt in 1517 in a sermon dated by the experts from the year 1512 or, more accurately in our opinion, from 1515. We must quote from it at this point:

> Someone may say to me: how criminal and scandalous are the fornication, the drunkenness, the passion for gambling, all the vices of the clergy! ... Scandalous indeed, I admit. They must be denounced, they must be abolished. But the vices you mention are visible to everyone. They are grossly material. Anyone can see them, and so they trouble men's minds. ... Alas! the evil, the plague that is incomparably more harmful and terrible, the silence organized about the Word of Truth and its adulteration, the evil that is not grossly material, this is not even noticed, nobody is shocked by it, no-one is terrified by it. ... How many priests will you find today who think it is less sinful to sin against chastity, to forget some prayer or other, to make a mistake in reciting the Canon of the Mass, than to neglect to preach and correctly interpret the Word of Truth? ... And yet the only sin a priest can commit, as a priest, is the sin against the Word of Truth (*Luther's Works*, Weimar edn I, 10–17).

What Luther said at this time was wise and correct up to a point. He was far from believing that the whole Church could be capable of this "adulteration" of the Word of Truth. But a few years later we find him believing and saying that he is the only interpreter of what he emphasizes is the "Word of Truth".

This then is the Protestant thesis in regard to the causes of the Reformation. It is the thesis of doctrinal corruption.

The Council of Trent, as we shall see, erected two defences against it: 1. the condemnation of the Protestant interpretations of the "Word of Truth" and hence the refusal to accept any adulteration of it in the Church; 2. the reform of abuses not in the sphere of doctrine but in that of canonical discipline.

Modern research has made a profound study of all this and replaced the two theses of doctrinal corruption and abuses by a broader, more complete view. It has examined the political, economic, intellectual, religious and moral causes.

In the political sphere, it is a striking fact that neither the pope nor the emperor were able to nip the revolt in the bud. Their power must therefore have lost much of its prestige. Luther, who was for a time egged on by poverty-stricken and rebellious knights, found a firm and lasting support in princes such as the elector of Saxony and the landgrave of Hesse who flouted the ineffective thunderings of the emperor. Zwingli, Calvin and Bucer were protected by the Councils of the cities which gave them a home. The same was the case with Oecolampadius and many others we shall mention.

From the economic standpoint, monastic property was a tempting booty for the shaky finances of States both great and small. Property in mortmain, it was said, would be put into economic circulation again whereas it was now static. This is a point that needs looking into much more closely. In any case the heavy burdens of the nations were not made any lighter, and the terrible Peasants' War made it abundantly clear to the unhappy serfs and freemen who worked on the land that they had been wrong to expect that the "Christian liberty" proclaimed by Luther would be extended to them also. The social structure did not change as a result of the Protestant "Reformation", nor, for that matter, as a result of the "Catholic Reformation".

Among the intellectual causes, we must point out the decadence of scholasticism which had been reduced to a monotonous and shallow game of words; the return to the sources recommended by the humanists; and especially the revival of biblical studies already evident in the cases of Erasmus, Lefèvre d'Etaples and Reuchlin, though inspired by ideals very different from those of Luther and Calvin.

Nevertheless it remains true to say that it would be absolutely wrong from the historical point of view to conceal under these general causes those which were more proximate and effective, namely, the personalities of the reformers themselves. Men like Luther, Zwingli and Calvin gave their "reformation" a decisive direction, varying it is true, in the case of each of them. These variations will have to be indicated later. Hence it is these "innovators", as the Catholics called them, who must be studied both in their lives and in their doctrines.

LUTHER (1483-1546)

Luther was born on November 10th, 1483 at Eisleben in Saxony. His father, a poor miner, seems to have left him nothing but a pugnacious and uncouth temperament. His mother, Margaret Ziegler, was not the sort of woman to spread joy in the family home. Martin Luther's youth was a cheerless one. He was scolded, punished and often beaten for mere trifles. It was doubtless from his mother that he inherited his marked taste for stories of diabolical activities and witchcraft. His school life was one long tale of privation until the moment when a generous woman, Ursula Cotta, gave him a home at Eisenach and became his adoptive mother. He was intelligent and a quick learner. His father, proud of his success, wanted him to study law. And so the young man followed the preliminary courses in the faculty of law at Erfurt University. He obtained the degree of master of arts. The future promised well for him. Then it was learned that he had suddenly entered the Augustinian friary. On July 2nd, 1505, he had been caught in a terrifying storm at the gates of Erfurt. He thought he was at the point of death and he had made a hasty despairing vow to become a monk if the lightning did not strike him. A fortnight later, he was as good as his word. This unpremeditated vocation was to weigh heavily on his whole life. He was fond in later years of saying that in the monastery he had been subjected to frightful penances, that he had mortified himself beyond all reasonable bounds. At the beginning of the twentieth century, a scholar of the front rank, Father Denifle, showed that Luther's statements are belied by all the authentic documents. Since then, the story of Luther's life has been studied by the critics. It is now admitted by everyone that Luther in his maturity became, as a Protestant author says, a myth even for himself.

On May 2nd, 1507 at the end of his novitiate, Luther was ordained priest. In 1508 his superiors moved him from Erfurt to Wittenberg. He was to teach in the University which had just been founded in the town. A journey he made to Rome in 1510–11 on the business of his Order had no disturbing effects (whatever he may have said to the contrary at a later date) on his attachment to the Roman Church and his obedience to the Holy See.

He continued to combine study with teaching and in 1512, to his great joy, he was awarded the cap of a doctor of theology. He remained very proud of this to the end. He then began to consider the Bible as his own personal domain, his private preserve. He plunged into it with delight. But his biblical study was not of the same kind as that of men like Erasmus and Lefèvre d'Etaples, his contemporaries. He read it with his own personal problems in mind. What he sought more than all else in it was comfort and spiritual security. In the Psalms, on which he wrote a commentary in 1514, he discovered nothing that was not already common knowledge in the Church. But when in 1515 he began to study St Paul's Epistle to the Romans he found in it meanings which he believed were entirely new and he constructed a doctrine so wonderfully suited to his own personal needs that he clung to it with all his strength until he reached the point at which he refused to renounce it. What then, was this doctrine?

LUTHER'S THEOLOGY

There are two essential points we must bear in mind regarding what was to become Luther's religion. The first is his view of *original sin*. For him it was not by any means what men had hitherto believed, namely, the loss of grace. No, it was quite simply the total corruption of human nature. Here is the definition he himself gives in his *Commentary on the Epistle to the Romans*:

> Original sin is the loss of all righteousness and of all the power possessed by our physical and mental faculties, both internal and external. It is our tendency to evil, our distaste for the good, our unwillingness to face the light and to follow wisdom, our love for error and darkness, our refusal to do good works and our loathing of them, our readiness to do evil.

In other words, Luther identifies original sin with *concupiscence* which is its consequence. From thenceforward he was in the throes of a fundamental pessimism and asserted that in men sin is incurable and indestructible. And this to such an extent that we commit mortal sin in all our acts, even, and above all, in those we believe to be the best, such as our acts of love of God. It follows that all men deserve hell, that salvation by works is impossible, that the law promulgated by Moses is impossible to obey in practice and that it is calculated only to plunge us into despair.

This is Luther's first description of the human condition. Here is the second: Among the mass of mankind condemned to damnation, God in his goodness, and for no other reason, chooses his *elect* and abandons the rest to the fate they deserve. This is known as *predestination*. Only Luther's disciples can claim a right to it. The elect are no more free than the reprobate. In his celebrated book *De Servo Arbitrio* (1525), Luther has one decisive sentence: "*God foresees, foretells and brings all things to pass. His predestination is like lightning which blasts and completely destroys human liberty.*"

But how does God set about saving his *elect*? It is perfectly simple. Into those driven to despair by the *law*, he suddenly instils his *Promise*. Over against Moses he sets Jesus Christ. A light is lit in the soul, the light of faith. And *faith without works* brings about *justification*. God considers as *justified* those to whom he has given faith and this without any merit or initiative on their part. This justification is not *interior*, it is entirely *exterior* in the sense that the just are *covered* by the cloak of the merits of Jesus Christ. All the elect are equal. They are all just men and sinners *at one and the same time*. Of themselves they are sinners, through Jesus Christ they are justified.

However, at the outset and until the year 1518, Luther had not yet discovered the inner nature of the faith which saves without works. This faith doubtless involves an acceptance of the teaching of the Gospel, but Luther does not want us to feel *secure*. No one knows whether he has faith or not. One of the reasons why he attacked indulgences was that they produce a sense of security. Men ought rather to "resign themselves to hell", since this is what they all deserve. It was not until 1518 after what has been called "the Experience in the Tower" that he suddenly realized that the *Promise* was unconditional, that faith in the Promise could be nothing other than *the certitude of personal salvation by faith without works*. Thenceforward he was in possession of a complete system. It was only to be amplified by later *ad hoc* conclusions. In 1519 the Councils were quoted against him. He rejected them on the grounds that they were fallible. The authority of the pope was quoted against him. He declared that the pope was anti-Christ. In 1520, he reduced the number of the sacraments from seven to two or three. In 1521, he rejected the sacrifice of the Mass and the monastic vows.

This theology therefore was built up of bits and pieces, as circumstances dictated. He himself said that it was due to his opponents that he had made so much progress.

But his break with the Church was gradual. At the outset and for several years later, Luther believed he was only

dealing with theological opinions and not in any sense with
the traditional faith of the Church. When eventually this
traditional faith was quoted against him, he answered that
the Bible alone, and the Bible as interpreted by himself, was
the source and the norm of all divine truth.

TOWARDS REVOLT AND SCHISM

The occasion of Luther's revolt was quite in keeping with
the spirit of the times. The policy of magnificence adopted by
the popes from the period of Nicholas V had been of great
profit to the artistic development of the century but it required a great deal of money. And so the Curia used every
means to acquire it. It sold dispensations at the highest possible price. It sold indulgences. This was certainly one of
the most regrettable abuses in the Church at the time. To
make possible the building of the basilica of St Peter's, an
indulgence was granted to the young Prince Albert of Hohenzollern. At the same time he purchased for a large sum the
dispensation needed for him to be simultaneously archbishop-
elector of Mainz, archbishop of Magdeburg and administrator
of the bishopric of Halberstadt. The preaching of this indulgence was entrusted to the Dominican John Tetzel, a popular
orator, adequately educated but with a tendency to boost
the promised indulgence by what were no more than theological opinions. For instance, one of the objections raised
against him was that he declared in his sermons that an indulgence applicable to the souls in purgatory was immediately
effective once the fixed sum was paid by way of alms:

> No sooner in the box you drop your mite,
> Than a soul from Purgatory to heav'n takes flight!

Tetzel's preaching shocked the public. Luther made it his own
opportunity to come forward as the champion of popular
grievances against the Roman Curia.

Hence on October 31st, 1517, he nailed to the door of the
collegiate church of Wittenberg ninety-five theses in which

he made a strong protest against the papal financial system. He said, for example: "The Church's treasury of indulgences is a net now used to fish for men's wealth"; "If the pope knew the extortionate demands made by the preachers of indulgences, he would sooner see the basilica of St Peter reduced to ashes than build it on the skin, flesh and bones of his flock."

Luther's action created an enormous impression throughout Germany and then through all Christendom. A storm of applause broke out whilst protests were also made against him. He had set light to the gunpowder.

Events now began to follow one another rapidly. Luther was not the sort of man to beat a retreat. He was urged on, in fact, by the neo-pagan humanists who were later to be his bitterest enemies. What angered him most was criticism from theologians. His replies were spirited and angry. He refused to go to Rome to prove his innocence. At Augsburg he faced Cajetan, papal legate, cardinal and a great Thomist theologian. After some heated discussion with him, he fled from Augsburg and appealed from the pope ill-informed to the pope better informed (October 22nd, 1518), and then from the pope to the Council (November 28th, 1518). All this he did before a notary. The matter of the indulgences soon became secondary. Luther's private theology, which we have already summarized, now came to the forefront. There was no longer any possible compromise between this doctrine and that of the Church. At the Leipzig Disputation (June 27th–July 16th, 1519), the Catholic theologian, John Eck, challenged Luther with several definitions made by Councils, particularly by the Council of Constance against John Huss. At this point, Luther made his repudiation of Councils as being liable to err. John Eck then replied amid the applause of the great majority of those present: "If you believe a properly consti-tuted Council is fallible and has in fact been mistaken, then for me you are no more than a publican and a pagan."

There could be no doubt that Rome would issue a con-demnation. A Bull from Rome, dated June 15th, 1520, condemned forty-one propositions in Luther's writings. Even before he knew its contents, Luther, Augustinian friar though he was, had written to a friend: "The die is cast. I despise for all eternity the fury or the favour of Rome." On July 17th, he made public the fact that he had received assurance of support from the knights, Silvester of Schaumberg and Franz of Sickingen. He at once set to work and on August 1st, 1520, published a manifesto entitled: *To the Christian nobility of Germany, on the Reform of the Christian State*. In it he declared that all Christians are equal by virtue of the universal priesthood, conferred on them at baptism. All can and ought to have recourse to the Bible alone as the source of truth. Emperors and princes have more right than the pope to convoke a general council.

In October 1520, he attacked the sacraments in his work *On the Babylonian Captivity of the Church*. He reduced them from seven to two, Baptism and the Last Supper, or to three at the most, by mentioning Penance with the others. But their efficacy depended entirely on faith which alone justifies. Finally, during November he brought out his third "reforming" book *On the Liberty of a Christian Man*.

Meanwhile, the Bull of Condemnation had arrived in Germany. To show his contempt for it, Luther publicly burned it in the presence of all his Wittenberg students on December 10th, 1520, and with it the *Corpus Juris* and the *Summa* of St Thomas Aquinas.

He was excommunicated on January 3rd in the following year. But the question was, how would the emperor proceed to execute the sentence? Charles V was young and self-willed. He soon made up his mind. He summoned Luther to the Diet of Worms where he was to be ordered to retract. After one day given over to reflection, Luther made the following declaration to the Diet. Its radical character is obvious:

Unless I am convinced by proofs from Scripture and by clear reasons—for I believe neither in pope nor in Council apart from the pope: both have certainly often erred and contradicted themselves—I am bound by the documents I have brought with me and my conscience is the captive of God's own words. I can retract nothing, because to go against conscience is both unsafe and unseemly. God be my help, Amen!

This declaration marks the beginning of the Protestant revolt.

THE ESTABLISHMENT OF A COUNTER-CHURCH

Luther had been placed under the ban of the Empire, that is, he had been outlawed. But, by virtue of his safe-conduct, he had to be brought back to Wittenberg. On the way he was mysteriously carried off by order of his sovereign, Frederick of Saxony. He was disguised, given the name of "George the Knight" and hidden in the Wartburg castle.

He remained there for ten months in great physical and spiritual suffering, working at his translation of the Bible. In his absence, his Wittenberg friends continued the separatist movement. Canon Carlstadt and the monk Zwilling led the revolt while young Melanchthon looked on, outflanked and powerless. In their sermons these two men called for a married clergy, the abolition of monastic vows and the Mass, and a general exodus from the religious houses. Luther approved from afar, but was irritated at seeing his party under the control of other men. Wittenberg was seething with excitement. Priests were marrying, monks leaving their monasteries and the ceremonies of the Mass were changed. Communion was given under both kinds without previous confession. Images and crucifixes were overthrown. But confusion reached its height when certain "prophets" arrived, claiming to be inspired by the Holy Spirit, and insisted that adults should be rebaptized, since infant baptism was invalid. These men were Anabaptists and their leader was Thomas Münzer. Eventually Luther, driven desperate by Melanchthon's appeals, could stand it no longer. He boldly left the Wartburg and returned to Wittenberg in spite of the sentence under

which he lay. He re-established order in the town after a
week of energetic sermons (March 1522). He claimed to be
the defender of law and order and the elector of Saxony
tacitly recognized him as such. Luther declared himself
totally opposed to the extremists Carlstadt, Zwilling and
Münzer, whom he called fanatics. He imposed his own
authority and soon expelled all who resisted him. The "liberty
of the Christian man" he had preached so often, was to be
buried under the régime of a State Church. All the districts
which later rallied to his teaching and broke with the pope,
followed his example. The new motto was to be *Cujus regio,
ejus religio*. Every man was to follow the religion of his
country, that is, of his ruler.

The terrible Peasants' Revolt, which claimed to base itself
on the Gospel, was wiped out in blood. Luther approved of
its suppression, using these sinister words: "My lords, deliver
us, come to our help . . . use the sword, cut as many throats
as you can. . . . An anarchist does not deserve to be reasoned
with, for reasons are just what he will not accept. Such
people must be answered by the fist. . . . Donkeys need beat-
ing and the common people need to be governed by force.
God is well aware of this for he has not given a fox's brush
to those who rule, but a sword." This kind of teaching
tended to inculcate the worship of force as a mark of divine
vocation.

During the Peasants' War, Luther, in spite of his vows,
had married a former nun, Catherine of Bora. She bore him
five children, three boys and two girls. Luther's last descen-
dant died in 1759.

ZWINGLI (1484–1531)

While Luther was completing the organization of his
Church and disposing of his opponents, Catholics on the
right and "fanatics" on the left, thus earning the title of the
"Pope of Wittenberg" which he was soon to be given, another

reformer arose in Switzerland. He was to become Luther's rival in biblical science and to cause him a great deal of trouble because of interpretations of the Bible in disagreement with his own. These divergencies were to produce what Bossuet at a later date called "The Variations of the Protestant Churches".

Ulrich Zwingli was born at Wildhaus on January 1st, 1484. Thus he was only six weeks younger than Luther. After studying at Berne, Basle and Vienna, in preparation for the priesthood, he had become parish priest of Glaris, then a military chaplain in Italy and finally parish priest of Einsiedeln. He had early shown a marked leaning towards literary studies. During his youth, his great hero was Erasmus. He prided himself on his ability to read the New Testament in Greek. This would have been impossible for Luther to do. Nothing suggested he would break with Rome when he became parish priest of Zürich in 1519. Although he always maintained he had learned nothing from Luther, he was among those who severely criticized the abuse of indulgences and he openly declared that he would only preach "the pure Gospel" by direct recourse to the biblical texts. There seems no reason to suppose he abandoned the "Erasmian reform movement" or adopted Lutheranism when the latter was condemned. His break with the Church was a gradual affair. He moved prudently and by carefully calculated stages. He began in 1522 by publicly attacking the practice of the Lenten fast, and in a letter to the bishop of Constance, his ordinary, asked for a married clergy. He himself in 1524 publicly married a widow with whom, to everyone's knowledge, he had been living. She bore him a child four months later. Meanwhile he had obtained the support of the Zürich Council composed of burgesses whom he called to witness his way of understanding the Bible. They naturally agreed with him on all points. Like Luther, therefore, though with obvious differences of method, he appealed to the laity against ecclesiastical authority. At his instigation the city Council ordered that all preaching in future was to be "according to the Bible only". It was also stipulated that no more help was to be given to "foreign" powers. This meant that Zürich would refuse to supply military recruits to France and to the Holy See. Thus Zwingli's sermons became increasingly radical. After celibacy of the clergy and fasting, he rejected the veneration of our Lady and the saints and denied the dogmatic authority of the pope and the Councils. He also forbade further veneration of "images". For him the Mass was not a sacrifice, it was merely a commemoration of Christ's Last Supper. But he was skilful enough to do all this as though forced into it by the text of Scripture. When he had prepared his public, and through it the City Council, he found ways of organizing "public disputations", that is, debates in which he had no difficulty in pulverizing his opponents since he could rely in advance on his audience which he had asked to give the verdict in the last resort. There was, for example, a debate on January 29th, 1523, then a second on October 26th–28th of the same year. On the latter occasion it concerned only the Mass and images. The "reform" in the Zwinglian sense was skilfully contrived. It was gradual and it worked under the patronage of the City Council. In March 1525, Zwingli published the only book in which his doctrine is systematically expounded, his *Commentary on true and false religion* (written in Latin).

Zwingli's position was now the following: he fought on three fronts, 1. against the Catholic tradition which would soon be eliminated either by consent or by force; 2. against the Anabaptists, who had become the nightmare of the "innovators" since they appealed to the masses of the people and, taking their stand on the Bible, proved far more revolutionary than Luther and Zwingli whom we may call the "reformers with a backing" since they enjoyed the patronage of the civil power; 3. against Luther himself with whom he disagreed on the subject of the sacrament of the Eucharist. Zwingli held the opinion of the Dutchman, Cornelius van

Hoen, and so rejected the "real presence". In his view, the words "This is my body", which have been understood in their literal sense since the very beginning of the Church and which even Luther himself understood (though doubtless in his own way) as having their literal meaning, were to be taken in a symbolic sense: "This is a symbol of my body".

But if Zwingli's victory, over the Catholics on the one hand and the Anabaptists on the other, turned out to be relatively easy, a violent dispute broke out between him and Luther. It is known to history as the Sacramental Quarrel.

The biblical creed common to the two "innovators" thus proved fallacious. On matters of primary importance, Zwingli and Luther put forward contradictory interpretations. The Protestant revolution, which had already been eroded by Anabaptist illuminism, now found itself divided into two. On the opposing side, the great strength of Catholicism then and down to our own days, was to be its doctrinal and disciplinary unity.

We add at once that the correspondence on their opposing views between Zwingli and Luther led nowhere. Each considered himself the victor and boasted of adherents rallying to his side from various quarters. The landgrave of Hesse made an unsuccessful attempt for purely political reasons to reconcile the two parties so that all the Protestants could be grouped into a League against the emperor who had remained faithful to Catholicism. The Marburg Colloquy in 1529 brought the two opponents together for several days but only served to accentuate their contradictory views. On the Zwinglian side, Luther was accused of making himself into a pope. On the Lutheran side, Zwingli was said to be suffering from megalomania. At the Diet of Augsburg, of which more will be said later, Zwingli produced a *Fidei ratio* which was received with disdain by the majority of those present (1530). In the following year Zwingli was killed at the battle of Cappel on October 11th, during a war between Zürich and the neighbouring Catholic cantons. When his body was found after the battle it was cut to pieces and burned. "Such was the end of the glory they sought for themselves by their blasphemies against Christ's Last Supper", declared Luther when he heard of the death of his rival and the humiliating peace treaty his supporters had had to sign. To the very end of his life he never ceased to say that Zwingli's death was a well-deserved chastisement for his incorrigible pride.

PROTESTANTISM AND THE DIET OF AUGSBURG

We have used the word Protestantism on many occasions when speaking of the "innovators" or "reformers", but we have done so by anticipation and because the word has become traditional. In actual fact, it only made its entry into history on April 19th, 1529, when the Diet of Speyer confirmed the decree of banishment issued at Worms in 1521 against Luther. It also forbade under the heaviest penalties any suppression of the Mass. It was then that the States which had already been won over to the new ideas presented a solemn *protest*, later changed into an "instrument of appeal", on April 25th. The signatories included five princes and fourteen towns in the Empire. As early as the year 1522, a certain number of those who were soon to be called "Protestants" had joined together in a secret League.

Later, the word was to have a wider sense as new forms of separatism appeared. For Bossuet in his *Histoire des variations des Eglises protestantes* (Paris 1688), there were four principal groups of "Protestants", the Lutherans, the Zwinglians, the Calvinists and the Anglicans. But on the fringe of these "established Churches" there had been from the beginning, and there were to continue to be in increasing numbers, marginal Churches or sects more or less persecuted by the others. We have already seen that this was the case with the Anabaptists. Today it is estimated that there are 250 Protestant denominations in the United States.

The original Protestant movement spread in two ways:

firstly, by means of the printing press, that is, through the writings of Luther, Zwingli and the other great leaders. These writings were carried to all parts by numerous *colporteurs*; secondly, by preachers in various localities whose allegiance had been won through these writings. Among these men particular attention should be drawn to apostate monks who formed the great majority of this class. Each operated in one city or one State, Lang at Erfurt, Henry of Zütphen at Bremen, Wenceslas Link at Altenburg, Güttel at Eisleben, etc. During the century, converts to Protestantism were to include a general of the Capuchins, Ochino, a bishop and former nuncio, Vergerio, a cardinal, Odet de Châtillon, and other persons of note.

The division between the Catholic Church and Protestantism was finally established by the failure of the Diet of Augsburg presided over by the Emperor Charles V in person. The Diet had opened on June 20th, 1530. The emperor, whose zeal for the faith was held in check by his fear of the Turks, by the strength of the dissidents which was already guessed at, since they were united in a secret League, and by his rivalry with France, proved much less threatening than the Lutherans had feared. Luther, under sentence of banishment, was safely guarded in the castle of Coburg. Acting in his name and in that of the dissidents as a whole, Philip Melanchthon had drawn up (with obvious attempts at compromise) a Confession of Faith, since known as the Augsburg Confession. It was presented on June 25th. It had been signed by seven princes and two imperial cities. Immediately three currents of opinion revealed themselves. The emperor and the Catholic princes were in favour of repression and Melanchthon's document was rejected. But a certain number of princes (and these included several bishops) were in favour of toleration, whilst a resolute minority publicly declared its acceptance of the dissident Confession. The emperor, still preoccupied with political calculations, decided that the Confession should be refuted by the Catholic theologians, that this refutation should be read to the dissidents and a summons addressed to them insisting on the suppression of all the doctrinal and liturgical innovations hitherto introduced, until a future Council should meet. Naturally the dissidents refused to make any concession. There were refutations from both sides and on September 22nd, 1530, the ordinance of the Diet referred the whole issue to a future Council although none was yet envisaged.

The Lutheran States replied quite simply by meeting on December 25th, 1530, at Schmalkalden, a little town in Hessian Thuringia, where they inaugurated for a period of six years the League of Schmalkalden which made Lutheranism a political and military force having at its disposal an army of 10,000 infantrymen and 2,000 horsemen. This was sufficient to make the emperor realize how powerless he was. Switzerland remained aloof, but Germany was divided into two irreconcilable camps. In time this fact was to give rise to a first series of wars known as the Wars of the League of Schmalkalden. The first of these was won by Charles V but the second he lost. This was followed by the Peace of Augsburg (1555). Then in the next century, came the terrible Thirty Years War (1618–48), which ended with the signing of the Treaty of Westphalia. But this takes us beyond the terms of reference of the present book.

CHAPTER V

CALVINISM TO 1564 AND

ANGLICANISM TO 1571

THE ORIGINS OF THE REFORMATION IN FRANCE

Even before Luther with his typically Saxon enthusiasm had given the reform movement in the Church the character of an insurrection and a revolution, a very active but more moderate group had come into existence in France under the guidance of the devout and learned Lefèvre d'Etaples (1455–1536) and the patronage of the generous-hearted Guillaume Briçonnet, future bishop of Meaux. This group held fast to the unity of the Church and wished at all costs to avoid any schism. It transferred its centre of operations to Meaux when Briçonnet became its bishop, and was known as the Meaux group. Beside Briçonnet and Lefèvre it included Gérard Roussel, future bishop of Oléron, Josse Clichtove who in 1524 wrote the first French refutation of Luther under the straightforward pseudonym of *Antilutherus*, Michel d'Arande, future bishop of Saint-Paul-Trois-Châteaux and Guillaume Farel, a restless and roving spirit who was finally to go over to heretical and schismatic Protestantism.

The Meaux group found favour with the sister of Francis I, Marguerite of Anjou, but it was attacked with the utmost vigour by the impetuous Noël Beda who was followed in this by the Sorbonne, at that time an antiquated institution. As early as 1521, the Sorbonne condemned 101 propositions taken from Luther's works. The Meaux group was soon accused of favouring heresy. Briçonnet had to publish two pastoral letters one after the other in order to demonstrate his innocence. Yet this did not prevent the Meaux group from finding itself obliged to disband. Some of its members remained Catholics, others went over to Protestantism and others again continued to hold a vague reformist view which the two other parties looked on with disfavour. There had been serious scandals, paintings of the Blessed Virgin had been defiled and smashed, and statues of the saints subjected to rough usage. A Council of the Sens province, held at Paris in 1528, condemned the Protestant errors by instancing long before Bossuet the "variations" among the dissidents. New outrages against the statues and pictures of the Blessed Virgin aroused public indignation. On April 17th, 1529, a knight, Louis de Berquin, who had perhaps been imprudent rather than blameworthy, was executed at Paris. In spite of repressive measures, small Lutheran groups were formed in the towns, at Meaux in particular. Hence Protestantism in France was known as "Lutheranism" until roughly the year 1550, when it was given the name of a French refugee who was to be placed alongside Luther and Zwingli as the third great reformer. He was John Calvin.

JOHN CALVIN (1509–64)

He was born on July 10th, 1509, at Noyon in Picardy. His father, Gérard Calvin, was almost a churchman since he held the posts of bishop's secretary and collector of church taxes. He was, however, too fond of litigation and he died excommunicate in 1531. His eldest son, Charles, became a priest and also died excommunicate in 1537. John was the second son. After a short period at school in Noyon, he received the tonsure at the age of nine. This meant that he enjoyed a small ecclesiastical benefice and later received one with the care of souls. He shared the revenues with the priest actually in charge. He himself never took major Orders. He was a parish priest in name only. At fourteen, he went to Paris with, the children of the Montmor family to study at the University. He was taught by the grammarian Mathurin Cordier and joined assiduously in theological discussion at the Montaigu College one of whose students was shortly to be Ignatius of Loyola. At that time Calvin was a severe, somewhat un- sociable young man. His fellow-students called him the "accusative" since he was fond of criticizing the faults of others. He was still deeply attached to the Catholic Church and to what he later called "the superstitions of the papacy". However, he abandoned his theological studies under pres- sure from his father, and applied himself to those of the law. He left the Montaigu College in 1528 and went to Orleans and then to Bourges where he met the Lutheran Wolmar in 1531. It was during this year that his father died. He now felt free to give up the law for literature. He therefore became a humanist and, in 1532, he was devoting all his time to a commentary on Seneca's *De Clementia*. As yet he showed no signs whatever of the reformer to come. It appears that it was at some time between August and October 1533 that he experienced what he subsequently described as a *sudden* change of mind. We do not know what were its root causes.

In any case, it is generally believed that it was he who composed for his fellow-scholar, the future physician, Nicolas Cop, the inaugural speech the latter had to make as rector at the beginning of the academic year, November 1st, 1533. In this speech, Calvin slipped in some sentences attacking the scholastic theologians and spoke of the contrast between the law and the promise. This was a clear reference to Luther's doctrine.

This event was decisive in Calvin's life. The ceremony was scarcely over when two Franciscans lost no time in denoun- cing Cop's speech to the *Parlement*. The king was away,.but the laws against heresy were categorical. The *Parlement* ordered an inquiry. Cop tried to face this ordeal but he was not the kind of spirit of which martyrs are made. He ran away taking with him the seal of the University. Calvin too must have felt he was in danger, for he prudently moved from the capital and went to Saintonge to stay with his friend Canon du Tillet. He doubtless hoped that there might still be a change of opinion in France. Nothing of the kind ensued. On May 4th, 1534, shortly before his twenty-fifth birthday, the date on which he was due to receive major Orders, if he wished to keep his benefice, he resigned his living, returned for a while to Paris, but finding it still somewhat unsafe for him, eventually went to Strasburg and then to Basle. In France Catholic opinion was outraged by the "Affair of the Posters". On the night of October 17th–18th, 1534, posters couched in the most abusive language (doubt-less from the pen of Antoine Marcourt, Neuchâtel Protestant preacher) were displayed in Paris and even at the doors of the royal palace. They denounced "the horrible, gross and intoler-able abuses of the papist Mass". This insult to the faith of Frenchmen gave rise to repressive measures of the utmost severity.

In Saintonge Calvin began to write a methodical account of his new faith. He finished the work abroad and published it in Latin at Basle in 1536 under the title *Christianae Religionis Institutio*. The book was only a small one but Calvin continued to revise and enlarge it. It was to be his life's work. The 1536 edition had a preface in the form of a letter to the king of France, dated August 23rd, 1535. In it Calvin defended his doctrine, openly declared that it was strongly opposed to the revolutionary ideas of the Anabaptists, and made a fierce attack on Catholic doctrine. He went so far as to say that for Catholic priests "their belly is their God, and cookery their religion". This set the tone for future polemics. Luther had been violent, but Calvin showed himself still more bitter and implacable. After his book was published Calvin left Basle and stayed for a while at Ferrara in the house of the duchess Renée de France, who was in favour of the new ideas. But two months later he set out again for Basle to make his home there. But on his way, he was persuaded to stop at Geneva by Guillaume Farel who was preaching Protestantism in the city, though with little success. Farel asked him to join in the battle.

CALVIN AT GENEVA

Calvin was to become the "pope of Geneva" just as Luther was the "pope of Wittenberg", just as Zwingli had been the "pope of Zürich".

In fact, he was at Geneva for two periods. The first only lasted three years, from 1536 to 1538, the second from 1541 to 1564, in which latter year Calvin died.

On January 16th, Farel and Calvin submitted to the Council of the Two Hundred for its approval their "Articles concerning the organization of the Church and public worship at Geneva". This was the outline plan of the famous "Ecclesiastical Ordinances" which Calvin, after a formidable struggle, was to succeed in imposing on the city whose relentless dictator he had become. We shall not go into the details of Calvin's activities at Geneva, but we must point out what was original in his religious ideas. He was well aware of the inadequacies of Lutheranism and he proposed to do all in his power to remedy them. In the first place, too little attention had been paid to public morals. In the Lutheran States, the *Visitations*, which Luther had asked his prince to institute, had revealed great abuses. The common people had been delighted to learn that men were saved by faith alone and that works were not required. The result was a wave of appalling immorality. There is abundant evidence to prove this, much of it provided by Luther in person. Calvin was determined to avoid any such scandals in his neighbourhood. He inserted in the ecclesiastical regulations a severe code of morals. He succeeded in performing a remarkable feat by emptying Communion of the real presence of Christ while making excommunication, that is, banishment from the celebration of the Lord's Supper, the form of punishment most feared by his followers.

Secondly, Calvin noticed that in the Lutheran States, whether the authorities were city councils or princes, God's ministers were too much under the thumb of the civil power. He took care therefore to set himself, in the name of God, above the civil power and to submit the magistrates themselves to the checks and censures of ecclesiastical authority, in short, to his own. Calvin succeeded in making the State the servant of the Church.

His mind filled with these ideas, he skilfully contrived to wait for a year and a half after his expulsion from Geneva in 1538, before returning to the city. Meanwhile he was asked to do so again and again. He also laid down his conditions in the most categorical manner before yielding to the requests which reached him. He returned to Geneva in 1541 and never left it again.

The only name for the system he established is a "theocracy". "The Calvinistic theory", as M. Choisy, a Protestant historian, has written, "brings into operation the government of the Bible, which is a document of the Divine Law." "None", says another Protestant historian, Walker, "can deny the simplicity and the grandeur of this concept, although it is very doubtful whether it is a true interpretation of the Bible, although, too, its full application to modern life, which is so individualistic and complex, is completely impossible." In fact, modern Calvinism has jettisoned Calvin's concepts on almost all these points.

In the religious sphere he professed absolute predestinationism and everybody now agrees that this dogma makes God the most intolerable of tyrants. He also threw over the principle of "private judgement" and refused to accept any interpretation of the Bible other than his own. In our day, private judgement has become the very law of Calvinistic Protestantism. On every occasion he displayed a most severe intolerance. He expelled from Geneva all who did not think as he did and executed without mercy those he declared to be heretics, as in the case of Gruet, beheaded on July 26th, 1547, and especially in that of the celebrated Michel Servet who was burned alive on October 27th, 1553. But now tolerance has become the general rule in Protestant as in Catholic countries, and Geneva has erected a memorial to Servet as an act of reparation to his memory.

As regards the organization of his Church, Calvin summed it up in the following sentences: "There are four kinds of offices instituted by our Lord for the government of his Church. They are first, the office of pastor, then that of teacher, then that of elder and fourthly, that of deacon. Hence therefore, if we wish to have a well-ordered Church and to maintain it in its entirety, we must adhere to this type of system."

Pastors: it is to be noted immediately that he says nothing of bishops, while Luther kept them under the name of "superintendents" which is simply a translation of the Greek word *episcopos.* For Calvin, pastors are commissioned to preach, to admonish, to administer the sacraments, which are two only in number, that is, Baptism and the Last Supper. Calvin demands that pastors should have a vocation comprising three elements: examination, legal status and induction.

Teachers: that is men who teach young persons in schools of various grades under the direction of the authority of the pastors.

Elders: the article dealing with these is the most novel and from it is derived the name Presbyterianism later given to Calvinism. The elders are persons of standing elected by the Christian community and they form the Church Session, which is entrusted with the task of "keeping its eye on everything". This means that it is to be vigilant in enforcing the code of morals. The Church Session includes *ex officio* all the pastors plus twice as many elders. At Geneva it began to function on December 15th, 1541. It met every Thursday. Its authority extended over everything, doctrine, morals, liturgy, and no one could be exempt from its decisions. It was through the Session that Calvin governed with sovereign power. This does not mean there were no struggles. He had constantly to face opposition and it was sometimes extremely violent. But Calvin, by dint of his tenacity and severity, overcame every obstacle.

"The total number of persons punished", says Walker, "increased considerably and there can be no doubt that this was due to his influence. Between 1542 and 1546, fifty-eight persons were condemned to death and seventy-six to banishment."

COMPARISONS

There is a very striking contrast between Luther, Zwingli and Calvin. Luther, as we have seen, was impulsive, violent, impetuous, passionate, virulent and active. But, except when indulging in his fits of anger against Rome and the papacy, he made no secret of his fundamental German good nature, his feeling for poetry and the arts and a rather childlike sensibility. In his everyday life he was what we should call a "very good fellow". His *Table Talk*, so varied and free, provides proof of this.

Compared with him Zwingli is a less pleasant figure. He was a bold, dominating, calculating, disdainful and occasionally cynical man. In any case he died too soon to leave his followers any very profound or influential memory of himself. Bullinger, who succeeded him, was quite undistinguished. Zwinglianism as time went on amalgamated more or less with Calvinism.

Calvin is very different from either of the others. Luther, who detested Zwingli, eventually became equally hostile to this other newcomer. Calvin's principal biographer, E. Doumergue, assures us that there is only one authentic portrait of Calvin, that in the Geneva library of which there are reproductions everywhere. There seems to be a genuine and close correspondence between the physical portrait of Calvin and his moral portrait as revealed in his numerous writings, words and acts. The angular, pointed face, emaciated and emptied, so it seems, of all fleshly substance, the sharp nose, the tight lips, the cold, piercing look, the thin beard, the withered parchment-like skin, all give the impression of the man as he was, with his acute intellect, his imperious, rigid logic, his austere temperament, his aloofness from earthly pleasures, his hardness of heart, his dominating, implacable character.

It must be pointed out in his defence that he was almost always a sick man, he was constantly subjected to criticism and argument, consumed with ceaseless work, by trouble and care. In 1559 he began to spit blood. He lost his wife, Idelette de Bure, soon after their marriage and then his only child. He himself died on May 27th, 1564. Luther had gone before him to the grave on February 18th, 1546, and Melanchthon in 1560.

THE ENGLISH SCHISM UNDER HENRY VIII

We have seen that Lutheranism began as a heresy and then ended by becoming a schism. In England the contrary was the case. The movement of separation from Rome began as a schism and eventually became a heresy. In origin it was the regrettable consequence of the evil passions of a king thwarted by the firmness of a pope.

Henry VIII ascended the throne in 1509. He was then a young, generous prince, fond of luxury and pleasure, a handsome and brilliant horseman, an accomplished athlete, very jealous of his authority and resolved to reign without restraint or control. His minister, Wolsey, supported him in his plans for autocratic rule, while not forgetting his own personal interests.

When Luther began his attacks on the Church's doctrine, Henry VIII wished to refute him in person in the matter of the sacraments. Pope Leo X even conferred on him the title of Defender of the Faith of which he was very proud (1512). But a few years later the sad business of the royal divorce began. Henry VIII had married his brother Arthur's widow, Catherine of Aragon, Charles V's aunt. This had required a papal dispensation. She had borne him five children, but only one survived, a daughter, Mary Tudor. From 1519 onward, the king flaunted his great moral laxity. After 1524 he began to neglect the queen. An almost demoniac passion (in the words of the historian Ludwig Pastor) for Anne Boleyn turned his mind towards divorce. But he met with inflexible opposition from the Holy See. He argued that Catherine of Aragon was his sister-in-law and that Pope Julius II, in fact, had no power to grant him a valid dispensation so that he might marry her. Hence his marriage was null and void. But it was no use. Pope Clement VII, who was far from being intransigent, could not yield when a principle as sacred as that of the indissolubility of Christian marriage was involved. He resisted the king. Henry VIII first blamed Cardinal Wolsey whom he held responsible for having failed in his diplomatic negotiations. He was banished to his diocese of York. Accused later of high treason he died, before he could be brought to trial, in 1530.

After Wolsey, power passed into the hands of the ambitious and authoritarian Thomas Cromwell, a careful student of Machiavelli. It was he who persuaded the king to adopt extreme measures. Catherine of Aragon was driven from the court. Anne Boleyn was installed in her place in August 1531. On January 25th, 1533, she was secretly married to the king. Meanwhile the archbishop of Canterbury had died. To replace him, Anne secured the appointment of her chaplain, Thomas Cranmer, who hastened to annul the king's first marriage and to ratify the second (May 25th, 1533). On June 1st, Anne Boleyn was crowned queen with great pomp and ceremony.

This was an intolerable scandal. On July 11th, the pope ordered Henry VIII to give up his evil ways under pain of excommunication. He restored all her rights to Catherine of

Aragon while her case was still *sub judice*. Henry VIII, like Luther before him, replied by appealing to the Council. But Rome gave its sentence on March 23rd, 1534, and declared that the first of the king's marriages alone was valid. The king then caused the Act of Supremacy to be passed and promulgated. It made final the Anglican schism (1534). In this Act, he declared that he was the head of the Church of the Realm and forbade all relations with Rome. He demanded that the clergy and the crown servants should take the Oath of Supremacy. To refuse was high treason. He thus made himself master of the souls and bodies of his subjects. The Act of Supremacy was supplemented by the Act of Succession which named Elizabeth, the daughter whom Anne Boleyn had just borne to the king, as successor to the throne, and required that every subject should take a second oath on this point. Finally, terrible laws concerning treason instituted a reign of terror throughout the Realm.

THE ENGLISH MARTYRS

The bishops and the clergy, secular and regular, submitted as a body to the sovereign's wishes. A few brave men however offered a heroic resistance and carried it to the point of martyrdom. The Carthusians, Houghton, Lawrence and Webster, the Brigittine, Richard Reynolds, the secular priest, John Hale, refused to acknowledge the king's religious supremacy. They were arrested, tried, condemned and subjected to the horrible punishment meted out to traitors. They were hanged, drawn and quartered on May 4th, 1535. As they were passing to their execution under the sinister walls of the Tower, a prisoner looked at them and, deeply moved, said to his daughter: "Lo, dost thou not see, Meg, that these blessed fathers be now as cheerfully going to their deaths as bridegrooms to their marriage?"

The prisoner was the famous Thomas More, former chancellor of the Realm. No figure in history is more engaging than his. As a distinguished humanist, a friend of Erasmus and the author of a celebrated book, *Utopia*, Thomas More had had a brilliant career. But he had not hesitated to tender his resignation to the king rather than approve the fatal policy the latter had initiated. All he desired was to live at peace far from the world and to devote himself to study. The king's anger would not allow him to do this. When More refused to take the Oath of the Act of Succession, he was arrested, thrown into the Tower, subjected to innumerable hardships and despoiled of all his goods (April 17th, 1534). Nothing could make him falter, neither the entreaties of his daughter nor the poverty of his wife now reduced to selling her clothes in order to live. Interrogated by Thomas Cromwell in person on April 30th, 1535, he replied: "I am the king's loyal subject. . . . I treat no man ill, I speak ill of no man . . . if that be not sufficient to save a man's life, I desire not to live more." When he was condemned, he protested thus: "For one bishop of your opinion, I have a hundred saints of mine; and for one Parliament of yours, and God knows of what kind, I have all the General Councils for 1,000 years; and for one kingdom, I have all the kingdoms of Christendom."

He was led to the scaffold on July 6th, 1535. It was unsteady. The martyr, keeping his typically English sense of humour to the end, said to the lieutenant: "I pray you, sir, see me safe up, and for my coming down let me shift for myself."

A fortnight earlier, the bishop of Rochester, John Fisher, confessor and counsellor of Catherine of Aragon, had also faced death equally courageously. Paul III had created him a cardinal while he was in prison. Henry VIII had immediately sworn that Fisher's head should fall before he received the hat. From the scaffold, Fisher also made his profession of the Catholic faith, then, falling to his knees, recited the *Te Deum* and the Psalm beginning: "O Lord, in thee have I hoped."

Pius XI canonized these two great heroes in 1935, the fourth centenary of their deaths.

HENRY VIII AND CATHOLIC DOGMA

The Anglican schism soon turned into a vast confiscation of Church property. The monasteries were entered, pillaged and sold. Their spoils enriched the Crown on the one hand and the country gentry on the other. The latter were to become in consequence the strongest supporters of the "Reformation".

On the other hand, Henry VIII was careful not to lay hands on dogma. He published three formulas in succession: the *Ten Articles* in 1536. These were rather vague but clearly Catholic in intention; the *Six Articles* in 1539. These are quite categorical; *The Erudition of a Christian Man* in 1543. The Lutherans were burned at the stake as heretics, and Catholics hanged, drawn and quartered as guilty of high treason.

Henry VIII died on January 28th, 1547. He had condemned two of his successive wives to death as well as twelve dukes and earls, 164 landowners, two cardinal archbishops, eighteen bishops, three abbots, 500 monks, including priors, thirty-eight doctors of theology or canon law.

ANGLO-CALVINISM UNDER EDWARD VI (1547-53)

Henry VIII had several children by his six wives. He regulated the order of succession to the throne in a series of Acts. After his death, Edward VI, the son of Jane Seymour, came to the throne at the age of ten. Until 1549 authority passed entirely to the duke of Somerset, the king's uncle, then to the earl of Warwick. The country rapidly moved towards pure Calvinism under the leadership of Cranmer, archbishop of Canterbury. Cranmer sent to the Continent for Protestant preachers: Martin Bucer from Strassburg, Bernardino Ochino, ex-general of the Capuchins from Siena, Peter Martyr, ex-Augustinian from Fiesole, John Knox, the future reformer of Scotland. From Geneva Calvin sent letters of encouragement. In 1549 the English learned what they were to believe with the publication of the first Prayer Book together with the

Forty-two Articles which were to take the place of Henry VIII's known as "the Whip with Six Cords". Under Warwick in 1552, this Prayer Book was replaced by another more tinged with Calvinism than the first. But the young king died on July 6th, 1533, and a Catholic reaction immediately became imminent.

RETURN TO CATHOLICISM UNDER MARY TUDOR
(1553–9)

Edward VI was succeeded by Mary Tudor, Henry's daughter by his first wife. She was therefore born a Catholic and had never ceased to be one. She at once released the Henrician bishops from prison and appointed Gardiner as chancellor. It was now the turn of the Lutheran and Calvinist heretics to fill the prisons. All Edward VI's religious statues were abolished and relations with Rome were re-established. Cardinal Pole, the Queen's cousin, till then outlawed and condemned in his absence, returned to his country with the title of papal legate. There was a certain amount of resistance which was severely repressed, although the figure of 279 executions during this reign is lower than that of the victims of Henry VIII, Edward VI and Elizabeth. Under Mary Tudor the most noteworthy victim was Thomas Cranmer who, from the Catholic point of view, had been the most guilty. He was burned at the stake on March 21st, 1556. There was reason to hope that peace would gradually be restored when Mary Tudor, broken-hearted at the loss of Calais in 1558, died on November 15th of the same year.

THE FINAL BREAK UNDER ELIZABETH (1558–1603)

Queen Elizabeth, who succeeded Mary Tudor, was the daughter of Henry and Anne Boleyn. She had been brought up under somewhat unfortunate conditions but had learned French and Latin, a little Greek, Italian and Spanish. She had a great love of the arts and literature as intellectual luxuries, but was almost wholly without any moral or religious sense. She was flirtatious, morally lax, cynical and cruel. For her, religion was only a cog in the political machine. One of her tricks in the diplomatic field was to pretend she was on the point of becoming engaged to the kings and princes whom she wished to win over to her schemes. She succeeded so well in persuading the king of Spain, Philip II, who had been Mary Tudor's husband, that he undertook negotiations in Rome with a view to stopping or deferring any measures against her. The English Catholics were more or less abandoned to their fate. Elizabeth was thus able to strengthen her position and to provide the kingdom with the religious organization it was to preserve, in spite of manifold difficulties, down to the present day.

She carefully preserved the episcopal system which Calvinist countries had suppressed. But the Catholic bishops were removed. A professed Calvinist, Matthew Parker, was appointed to the See of Canterbury. He had himself consecrated according to the Ordinal of Edward VI by a bishop whose orders were doubtful. Parker in his turn consecrated the new bishops in accordance with the same Ordinal. This explains why Leo XIII, after a close examination of the historical circumstances of these ordinations, declared in the Bull *Apostolicae curae* (September 13th, 1896) that Anglican ordinations are invalid.

As early as the year 1559, Elizabeth had restored the Oath of Supremacy which made her the head of the Anglican Church, and then the Act of Uniformity, which brought the Prayer Book of 1552 back into use. The Forty-Two Articles however were reduced to thirty-nine. These have remained the profession of faith of the official Church of England. We say the official Church for there have never ceased to be groups of dissidents—dissenters—whose views have been to the left of those of the Established Church. These groups in most cases were persecuted as fiercely as the Catholics.

THE THIRTY-NINE ARTICLES

Among the Thirty-Nine Articles, which regulate the faith of the Anglican Church, a large number are orthodox, those, for example, concerning God, the Trinity, the Incarnation, Christ's death and resurrection, the Godhead of the Holy Spirit, the obligatory nature of the Decalogue, the Apostles', Nicene and Athanasian Creeds. But others are tainted with Lutheranism or Calvinism. Article 6 declares that Scripture contains all things necessary to salvation. Article 8 defines original sin as a corruption of human nature persisting even in those who are regenerated by baptism. Article 11 teaches justification by faith without works. Article 19 declares that the Church of Rome has often erred, even in matters of faith. Article 22 gives as examples of these "errors", the Catholic doctrines of purgatory, indulgences, veneration of images, relics and the saints in general. Article 25 only recognizes two sacraments, Baptism and the Last Supper. In the Eucharist, the Anglican Church with Calvin admits that the real presence is spiritual only and not substantial, and that it exists only at the moment of communion. Article 31 suppresses the Mass as a sacrifice and article 22 abolishes ecclesiastical celibacy.

The Thirty-Nine Articles adopted by Convocation (the Assembly of the Clergy held from January 13th to April 10th, 1563) were therefore by way of a compromise. They had the character of an agreed settlement, a vague and elastic happy medium. This was the ideal scheme for Elizabeth who was herself a sceptic. In this sense Anglicanism was clearly distinct both from Lutheranism and Calvinism whose areas of development we shall study in the next chapter.

CHAPTER VI

THE PROGRESS OF

PROTESTANTISM TILL 1618

IN GERMANY

We have followed the history of Lutheranism in Germany down to the formation of the Schmalkaldic League in 1531. Luther himself, though still under the ban of the Empire, was safe from any attack from the emperor or the pope. He lived for the rest of his life in Wittenberg at the Black Monastery, the religious house in which he had been a friar, presented to him by the elector in 1523. He lectured at the University and preached, but above all devoted himself to writing—letters to people in various parts of the Continent and also polemical or exegetical books. He was surrounded by admiring disciples, who have preserved for us his strange *Table Talk* in which serious and comic remarks are mingled with trivialities and even obscenities. It is here especially that we must see the "reformer" in his different capacities, as a religious leader, a controversialist, the father of a family and a biblical theologian. It is in his *Table Talk* that he gives his own definition of himself: "I am a rustic, hardheaded Saxon." His friends often said of him that he was "German to the core"—*kerndeutsch*.

Among his books, those to which he himself attached the greatest importance were his *De Servo Arbitrio*, written as an attack on Erasmus in 1524, and his *Small and Great Cate-*

chism published in 1529. He was not at all satisfied with the Augsburg Confession drawn up by his friend Melanchthon. He considered it too conciliatory and provided a summary of his own doctrine in the *Schmalkaldic Articles* (1537).

It was at Schmalkalden that he fell ill and, thinking himself at the point of death, left as a watchword for his followers the angry cry: "God fill you with hatred of the pope!"

He died of apoplexy on April 18th, 1546 at Eisleben, his native town. The story of his supposed suicide, propagated in Catholic circles, is a legend with no foundation in fact.

The expansion of Lutheranism in Germany took place principally in the following two ways: through the activity of Luther's disciples almost all of whom were, like himself, apostate religious or at least priests; by the process of secularization. This meant that great ecclesiastics, bishops, abbots or religious dignitaries declared themselves Lutherans and constituted themselves heirs to the Church property they had acquired by their election or appointment to a position among the Catholic clergy. Such property they then appropriated to themselves. One of the first of these secularizations had been brought about by the Grand Master of the Teutonic Order, Albert of Hohenzollern, who married in spite of his vows and founded the duchy of Prussia. After many ups and downs, and at the end of the two Schmalkaldic Wars, as they are called, the Peace of Augsburg (September 25th, 1555) laid down that there should be absolute mutual toleration as between Catholics and Lutherans; no other religious body was to be tolerated, least of all Calvinism; all secularizations previous to 1552 should be recognized; all future secularizations were prohibited by virtue of the "Ecclesiastical Reservation"; princes of the Church were to exercise no spiritual authority over their Lutheran subjects.

In actual fact, the "Ecclesiastical Reservation" was so badly observed that from 1555 to 1618, when the Thirty Years War broke out, no less than two archbishoprics and thirteen bishoprics had been unlawfully seized and secu-

larized by the Lutherans. In fact, this was one of the chief
causes of the war which ravaged Germany until the Treaties
of Westphalia in 1648.

OUTSIDE GERMANY

Although Lutheranism spread chiefly in Germany, it was
not long before it reached the Scandinavian countries. But
there politics played a greater part in its expansion than
did religious controversy.

In 1397, Queen Margaret of Norway had brought about
the union of the three crowns of Denmark, Norway and
Sweden in her own person. But this union of three nations
of very different stamp was to prove ephemeral. Sweden,
which considered itself the victim of the arrangement, provided itself with a king in 1448. He made the mistake of
trying to lay hands on Church property and was overthrown
in 1457. His place was taken by Charles I of Denmark who,
shortly after, obtained the crown of Norway for his own son.
The Swedish nobility was impatient under a foreign yoke.
Christian II of Denmark landed in Sweden, forced the archbishop of Upsala to crown him and attempted to impose his
authority by force and by executing the chief supporters of
the movement for independence. This is known as the massacre of Stockholm and took place on November 8th, 1520.
At this point Gustav Wasa appeared on the scene. His own
father had been among those massacred. He put himself at the
head of the exasperated patriots. His hatred of the Danish
king was linked in his mind with his hatred of the pope, for
Christian II seemed, since it was in his interest for the time
being, to lean on the support of the Catholic clergy. Gustav
Wasa won the day. Christian II was driven out and Wasa
became king in 1523. He made it his first concern to encourage
the spread of Lutheran ideas which the brothers Olavus and
Laurentius Petri, former Wittenberg students, had been already propagating since 1519. The new king coveted the

wealth of the clergy—seven bishoprics and fifty monasteries
—with which he could pay his war debts and consolidate his
somewhat shaky throne. A solemn disputation, in the style
then popular in many places, took place at Upsala on December 27th, 1524, with the object of obtaining a victory for the
Lutherans and so detaching the people from Rome. The
ceremonies of public worship were altered as little as possible
in order not to shock public opinion. Dogmatic discussions
were above the heads of the common folk. In 1527, Lutheranism, in a form adapted to the needs of the country was
declared the State religion, ecclesiastical property was confiscated for the use of the Crown. New bishops were chosen
from among the Lutherans. All Catholic resistance was wiped
out in blood.

Meanwhile, Christian II, hesitating between Catholicism
and Lutheranism as circumstances varied, bequeathed his
throne to his son Charles III who had become a convert to
Lutheranism and was casting envious eyes on the property
of the Church. On August 11th, 1536, he had all the bishops
arrested, and abolished the Catholic episcopate. He then sent
for an intimate friend of Luther, the former Premonstraten-
sian Bugenhagen, to organize the Danish Church. Bugenhagen arrived in July 1537. On August 12th, he solemnly
crowned the king and queen of Denmark and, although only
a priest, did not scruple to consecrate on September 2nd, seven
renegade priests as "superintendents", that is, as Lutheran
bishops. He then organized the liturgy and restored the University of Copenhagen, by appointing none but Lutheran
professors.

Charles III also imposed Lutheranism on Norway by force.
He had united this kingdom to Denmark by proclamation
on October 30th, 1536. His authority was immediately
acknowledged in the southern part of the country. But Olaf,
the Catholic archbishop of Trondhjem, who had four suffra-
gans in Norway and two in Iceland, put himself at the head
of the national resistance. Unfortunately he was obliged to

flee before the troops of Christian III when they disembarked at Bergen. All the bishops were arrested and the properties of their churches confiscated. The Catholic hierarchy was replaced, as in Denmark, by Lutheran superintendents (1537). To keep the people quiet, the same policy was followed as in Sweden, and as many as possible of the former ceremonies kept as they were in Catholic days. The change to schism and heresy took place almost unnoticed.

Finally, in Iceland, a dependency of Denmark, the same change was effected by a "Lutheran" appointed to the See of Skalholt in 1540. The Catholic bishop of Holum, John Aresen, attempted to resist the innovations, but he was beaten, arrested and beheaded on November 7th, 1550. After him, the last representatives of Catholicism in Iceland disappeared in 1552.

THE SPREAD OF CALVINISM

While Lutheranism was carving out territory for itself in the German and Scandinavian countries, Calvinism was engaging in still more successful activity. We have seen how, under Edward VI, it had almost laid hands on England. However, Anglicanism eventually took its place. We shall now follow its development in Switzerland, France, Scotland, the Low Countries, the Palatinate, Hungary and Poland.

Switzerland

Before Calvin, Swiss Protestantism had been predominantly Zwinglian. Zwingli's sacramental doctrine had provoked opposition in many quarters. We know that Luther had violently rejected it. And Calvin too found it superficial and even wholly secular. Zwingli's place was taken by Bullinger and there was an exchange of views between him and Calvin. After a visit from the latter in company with Farel, Zwinglianism and Calvinism were reconciled. In May 1549, the negotiations led to the *Consensus Tigurinus* or Zürich Agreement which in practice set the seal on the union of these two branches of the Reform. In Switzerland Catholicism remained as the creed of the cantons of Fribourg, Soleure, Uri, Schwytz, Unterwalden, Lucerne and Zug. On the other hand, Berne, Zürich, Basle, Schaffhausen and above all Geneva were bastions of Protestantism.

France

The resolute attitude of the Sorbonne and the support given by the clergy to the decisions reached at the Councils of Sens (held in Paris) and Bourges in 1528, were the preponderant factors here. Lutheranism was not wanted because it destroyed Catholic unity and created a lamentable confusion in the realm of doctrine. It continued to produce "variations" (a sure sign of error) and it was opposed to established dogmas and devotions dear to the French, in particular devotion to the Eucharist and to the Blessed Virgin. Protestantism had only succeeded in spreading in the suburbs of certain towns such as Meaux, Paris, Noyon, Amiens, Alençon, Bourges, Orleans and Poitiers.

Calvin had no hesitation in directing the French "Reformation" from Geneva. He trained preachers whom he sent secretly to various destinations according as the need arose. He wrote letters to the "reformed" groups exhorting them to persevere in spite of laws and persecutions.

Among the lower clergy and the monks there was a fairly large number of defections. Repressive measures which were mild enough under Francis I became very severe under Henry II. But the Calvinists went to their death with intrepid courage and a kind of sombre joy. They were convinced they were following in the footsteps of the martyrs of the early Church. Nor were they content merely to glory in their martyrs, they also indulged in aggressive acts and iconoclasm.

The foundation of the Calvinist Churches took place in two stages. There were embryo and fully-grown Churches. In the former, the members met in secret to read the Bible and

Calvin's letters, but there was no organization. In the latter, there were, as at Geneva, elected pastors, elders, deacons and a Session. Towards 1556–8 this constitution was set up and functioning in some fifty towns.

The total number of Calvinists in these Churches may have reached some 3,000,000 at the outside out of a total of 20,000,000 Frenchmen. But this was sufficient to form a threat to national unity. Henry II's violent repressive measures had no effect. On May 9th, 1558, the minister Macar who had just settled in Paris was able to say in a letter to Calvin: "In all parts of the kingdom, the fire has been lit and all the water of the sea would not be sufficient to put it out." And on May 25th, 1559, the first Calvinist Synod to be held in France was able to assemble in secret at Paris. It drew up the forty articles of the *Confessio Fidei gallicana*.

It was at this time that a very serious development took place. Persons of the highest rank in the State brought to Calvinism the prestige of their name and their influential support. Among these were the king of Navarre, Antoine de Bourbon, and his brother, the prince de Condé, great lords such as François de Châtillon and his two brothers, Admiral Coligny and Cardinal Odet de Châtillon. King Henry II took fright at this and hastened to make peace with Spain so that he might have his hands free. After his death during a tournament, the Wars of Religion broke out. They were chiefly political, wars of minorities and vendettas between different lords. During them there occurred assassinations and the abominable massacre of St Bartholomew (August 24th, 1572). In all there were eight devastating wars. It was only when Henry IV was converted to Catholicism that the French were once more united. The Edict of Nantes (April 13th, 1598) gave the dissidents a political status and at the same time established the fact of their defeat, to which Richelieu was to add the final touch by the capture of La Rochelle followed by the Edict of Alais in 1628.

Scotland

The propagator of Calvinism in Scotland was John Knox. Born at Giffordgate, Haddington, in 1505, he became a priest in 1530. His study of the Bible gradually converted him to Zwinglian ideas. After 1542, he had completely abandoned the Roman Church. His master, George Wishart, well known as an agitator, was burned at the stake on March 1st, 1546, and the dissidents assassinated David Beaton, the archbishop of St Andrews, on May 29th. John Knox had been the chief instigator of the murder. He was arrested and sent to the galleys at Rouen (1547–9). When he came out of prison he was summoned to the court of Edward VI by Cranmer and was able to preach Calvinism openly in England. After the young king's death he fled and took refuge at Geneva. He then became a fervent disciple of Calvin and translated the Bible. He kept in secret touch by letter with the dissidents in Scotland who in 1557 formed a League whose object was to destroy "the Synagogue of Satan", that is, Catholicism. The League appealed to him for active help.

Knox at once set out and landed at Edinburgh on May 2nd, 1559. By the 11th of the same month he was preaching at Perth and in such violent tones that the crowd took immediate action, rushed to the monasteries in the town, took them by storm and made a bonfire of the pious objects and pictures it found there. This was the beginning of a civil war. The regent of Scotland, Mary of Lorraine of the Guise family, was forced to take refuge in Edinburgh Castle. Her death in 1569 enabled the Protestant party to set itself up as the national party and to demand the withdrawal of all foreign troops, both French and English. A Scottish Parliament assembled. On August 17th, 1569, it adopted a Confession of Faith, *Confessio scotiana prior* (1560) (the *Confessio posterior* followed in 1561). Finally, on August 24th, it abolished the Mass and papal jurisdiction.

The *Confessio* had been drawn up by John Knox. He thus followed in his master's footsteps. If possible, he was even more sombre and inflexible than Calvin, had an even greater hatred of Roman customs, and was even more intransigent and pretentious in his dogmatism. He copied the Genevan pattern and established pastors, teachers, elders and deacons. But he did allow superintending pastors who were a pale reflection of bishops. Knox's institutions were to govern the Church of Scotland until 1645 when they were replaced by the Westminster Directory. After Knox's death, Calvinist radicalism became even more marked. Scotland was subjected to a strictly Presbyterian system, that is, it opposed anything remotely resembling episcopacy. It consisted in complete domination by Sessions in which the "elders" formed the majority. Hatred of Catholicism became an obsession and was stirred up by the fierce nature of the political struggle. The unhappy Queen Mary Stuart was dethroned, forced to take refuge in England where the astute Elizabeth kept her in prison for eighteen years and eventually sent her to the scaffold on February 8th, 1587.

The Low Countries

The history of the introduction of Calvinism into the Low Countries is scarcely less dramatic than that of its entry into Scotland. The Low Countries (now Holland and Belgium) belonged to the Spanish branch of the House of Austria. Charles V had repressed Protestantism in this area all the more rigorously in that it had caused him so many difficulties in Germany. But on October 26th, 1555, he had renounced the throne in the Low Countries in favour of his son, Philip II. The reserved, cold and haughty character of this prince soon made him as unpopular as his father had been the opposite. He was known to harbour an implacable aversion to Protestantism. The national opposition to the Spanish rulers therefore quite naturally adopted the form and the appearance of a struggle for religious independence. Philip II's measures against Calvinism soon provoked an insurrection. In November 1565, the Protestant League of Breda was formed. Three hundred gentlemen boldly came forward to present their demands to the regent, Margaret of Parma. One of the councillors, Count de Berlaymont, so the story goes, advised her to take no notice of these "Beggars". The malcontents gloried in this insult. What is certain, however, is that it was the fashion among them to carry the bag and the bowl, the beggars' badge. The terrified regent yielded and the "Beggars" won the day.

But the king held his ground and refused to withdraw his edicts. There were riots at Antwerp, Valenciennes, Saint-Omer and elsewhere. The Protestants attacked the churches and sacked them. The Catholics, who had originally joined the League of Breda, men like the duke of Egmont, now withdrew from it. To put an end to the rising, Philip II sent the fierce duke of Alba with a fleet and an army. He was given the task of crushing Calvinism (1567). But the reign of terror he introduced into the Low Countries provoked a general revolt of the United Provinces and the young William of Orange became its leader. A war of independence, often marked by great atrocities, then broke out in 1572 between the Calvinists and Spain. On January 23rd, 1579, Holland proclaimed her independence and eventually forced Spain to recognize it during the following century.

Following the example of the other Calvinist countries, those of the Low Countries had drawn up a Confession, the *Confessio belgica*, in 1561. From 1573 onward, Catholic worship was forbidden under pain of death in the provinces under their control, and the churches were changed into Protestant meeting places. There were executions, among them especially that of the nineteen Gorcum martyrs who were put to death in 1572. The Lutherans and those who favoured toleration were treated as on a par with the Catholics. The Universities of Leyden, founded in 1575, and Franeker (1585) became the intellectual centres of Calvinism. At Leyden, two equally famous teachers, Arminius and Gomar, adopted different views on the Calvinist doctrine of predestination. Arminius (1560–1609) interpreted it in the sense adopted by the majority of present-day Calvinists and so recognized the existence of human freedom. Gomar doggedly upheld integral Calvinism and absolute predestination apart from all question of merit. After Arminius's death, his supporters presented a *Remonstrance* which Gomar opposed with all his force. The Arminians were severely condemned at the Synod of Dordrecht (1618) but the struggles produced in the end a kind of religious indifferentism. This reaction caused the Low Countries to become at a later date the bastion of toleration and the printing and distribution house of all books under suspicion elsewhere.

In the Palatinate

On the strength of the principle *Cujus regio, ejus religio* Calvinism replaced Lutheranism when the Count Palatine, Frederick III (1559–76), adopted Calvin's principles and imposed them on his subjects in 1563. Pictures in the Protestant places of worship were destroyed, Lutherans were persecuted with the same severity as Catholics, and the Calvinist Heidelberg Catechism was made universally obligatory as a Confession of Faith. Under Louis VI (1576–8) there was a no less violent return to Lutheranism. But this prince's reign was very short and under his successor, Frederick IV, Calivinism triumphed. The Elector Palatine was to be the ill-starred champion of Calvinism during the first period of the Thirty Years War (1618–24). Later this area was to revert in part to Catholicism.

Hungary

This unhappy country, which had once been profoundly Catholic, had fallen victim to the Turks. Her soil was constantly trodden by the opposing Christian and Moslem armies. The Hapsburgs tried to subject it to their domination under the banner of Catholicism, but a national dynasty resisted their designs. Under cover of these struggles, Protestantism had no difficulty in introducing itself into the country under a Lutheran form to begin with. A certain John Houter, who was a grammarian, printer, geographer and publicist, set himself up as a reformer and, from 1542 onward, modelled himself on his Wittenberg forerunner. In 1550 or thereabouts, Hungary seemed to have gone over to Lutheranism. But a man named Matyas Devay, who had begun by being a follower of Luther at Wittenberg and had even lodged at his house, made contacts with the Swiss sacramentarians and then joined the Calvinists. Luther opposed him as a renegade, in his usual vigorous manner, from 1544 onward. A racial question then added further complications to the religious problems. The Germans with John Houter clung to Lutheranism and the Magyars with Devay to Calvinism. And as Calvinism thus took on a national character, it quickly won the day against Lutheranism. In 1577 the Synod of Czenger published a Confession known as the *Czengerina* which was ratified by the Synod of Debreczin in 1567. Nevertheless Catholicism put up a vigorous defence under the powerful influence of the archbishop of Gran, Nicolaus Olahus (1553–68). It recovered most of the lost ground during the next century.

Poland

Since 1525 Poland had been the scene of anti-Catholic movements. The Grand Master of the Teutonic Order, as we have seen, had become secularized in 1525 although remaining the vassal of Poland. King Sigismund I (1506–48), however, was a good Catholic and resisted to the best of his ability the progress of Protestantism in his dominions. This progress was encouraged by the almost total independence of the nobles. The great defender of Catholicism at this period was Laski, archbishop of Gnesen (1456–1531), but his own nephew, John Laski the younger (1499–1560), was to go over to Calvinism. Under King Sigismund II, the last of the Jagellons, and a fickle, weak ruler (1548–72), the number of dissidents increased. Each great nobleman desired to possess his "reformer"; Lutherans, Calvinists and Socinians (a rationalist sect founded by Faustus and Lelius Socinus, Italian refugees) waged bitter warfare against each other. However, the Synod of Sandomir, held on April 14th, 1570, succeeded in establishing peace between the various kinds of Protestants, who were reinforced at the time by the Brethren of Bohemia, descendants of the Hussites. The Confession of Sandomir or *Consensus Poloniae* was in fact Calvinist. The Catholic restoration was fortunate enough to have an energetic champion in Cardinal Hosius who was assisted by St Peter Canisius of the Society of Jesus, of whom we shall have more to say later. Poland then recovered herself and remained fundamentally Catholic.

MYSTICISM AND SCEPTICISM

On the fringe of the great Protestant sects, there grew up minor ones among which two extreme tendencies in the anti-Roman revolution became evident. These tendencies were mysticism and rationalism or scepticism. Anabaptism is typical of this mysticism. It was one of the causes of the terrible Peasants' War (1524–5). Efforts were then made to establish it at Münster under the leadership of "prophets" who claimed to be inspired by God. Anabaptism was crushed with extreme severity in 1534. The Anabaptists were the communists of the period. Later they sobered down and moved towards a pacifist form of Puritanism without any dogmas (Mennonites).

Socinianism, which started from the opposite point of view, found itself, with its founders Faustus and Lelius Socinus, hunted and driven out everywhere. It claimed to interpret Scripture solely by the light of reason and it was thus led to deny the Trinity and other mysteries of faith. As we have seen, it made some progress in Poland. But subsequently it was in the United States especially that all the various forms of Protestantism, from those which made the greatest claim to divine illumination to those which were the most rationalist, found refuge and never ceased to add to the number of "denominations" down to our own days. The principle of the appeal to the Bible alone was to prove beyond all doubt a source of division among Christians.

It is with this chaos of belief in mind that we must now examine the decisive strengthening of unity in Catholicism, for this was to give rise to the only true Reformation.

CHAPTER VII

SPONTANEOUS REFORM

A NECESSARY CLARIFICATION

Before we begin to describe the Catholic Reformation, one point must be made quite clear. Historians have become accustomed to use the word "Reformation" in their account of the various phases of the Protestant revolt, and the word "Counter-Reformation" to describe the Catholic revival. This way of putting things cannot be accepted by a Catholic. It presupposes three stages in the course of events.

At the first stage we find a Church full of abuses of every kind. It is in an exhausted and almost moribund state and is governed by popes who are no longer much more than brilliant Italian princes, subtle diplomats like Alexander VI or men of war like Julius II. It is in the hands of a thoroughly worldly episcopate, kept in a state of gross superstition by a crowd of degenerate monks who have long since lost the spirit of Francis of Assisi, Dominic, Bernard and others like them. Finally, its education is entrusted to universities in which an accumulation of glosses and commentaries has ended by arresting the forward movement of religious thought and extinguishing the very light of the Christian intelligence. At the second stage, the Middle Ages are dying when suddenly, in the dark and thundery sky, the storm breaks in 1517. A friar rises in anger and protests against the exactions and the tyranny of the popes. He rouses the Christian conscience against Rome, overthrows outmoded traditions and

ingrained routine, lifts up the Bible in a century that has
fallen into torpor and sleep, and lets loose the torrent of
God's Word across plains littered with scholastic speculation.
The voices of other brave men join with his, those of Zwingli
at Zürich, Bucer at Strasburg, Oecolampadius at Basle and a
little later that of Calvin, a genius who contributes his own
typically French clarity, logic, penetrating mind and his gift
for organization.

At the third stage, contrary to all expectation, the Catholic
Church reacts to the shock of the Protestant revolution and at
long last awakens, the religious orders begin to flourish again,
the Jesuits take the stage and the papacy itself is forced to
yield to pressure from all sides. The Council of Trent, in
spite of considerable difficulties, is assembled, Catholic discipline is restored, the seminaries are founded, the Protestant
flood is contained. The Counter-Reformation has saved the
Church. And all this is achieved at the cost of terrible wars
in Germany and France.

Certain historians have gone still further and insinuated or
roundly stated that the Church of the Council of Trent is very
far from being a continuation of the Middle Ages; the religion
of Ignatius of Loyola or Bossuet has only a distant resem-
blance to that of Thomas Aquinas or Bonaventure. The label
is the same, but the spirit has changed.

All this, however, is a baseless assumption. We are convinced that the Middle Ages did, on the contrary, continue
their line of development without any important change of
direction, and that our religion is in fact that of Bernard,
Francis, Dominic, Thomas and Bonaventure. Never at any
time was there any break or discontinuity. As proof of this,
we shall give a summary account of the "spontaneous reform"
within the Church. The powerful vitality of the Church in
the sixteenth century is revealed by the great number of saints
it produced and by the formidable spread of the Catholic faith
through its foreign missions in America and the Far East.

THE ORATORY OF DIVINE LOVE

Before Luther was heard of, devout and enthusiastic groups were formed within the Church. They were known as Brotherhoods, Confraternities or Societies of Divine Love. In Rome itself we find the Oratory of Divine Love. The movement began in Genoa among the friends of St Catherine Fieschi. Its founder was a layman, Ettore Vernazza (1470–*circa* 1524), notary and humanist, an indefatigable promoter of charitable works and founder of a hospital for incurables.

The Oratory of Divine Love at Rome probably dates from just before 1515. It soon spread to Vicenza, Venice, Naples and other places. At first, these groups were composed of fervent layfolk though they included a few priests. Each group had between forty and sixty members only. Among them were admirable men in whom we recognize the first true Catholic "reformers". Their spirit is entirely different from that of the Protestant "reformers". We may mention the gentle and generous Cajetan of Tiene (1480–1547). At his side was his inseparable companion, Giovanni Caraffa, bishop of Chieti (Theatum) from 1504, an impetuous Neapolitan and full of zeal. He was to become pope under the title of Paul IV. Together they founded a Congregation of "Regular Clerks", the first of its kind, to give an example to the "clerks" who on occasion were very far from regular. The congregation was to take the name of Theatines. These were never very numerous but so edifying and successful that they produced more than 200 bishops devoted to Catholic reform. All this movement prior to or contemporary with Luther was rooted in the medieval Church and owes nothing to the Protestant rebellion.

The Barnabites, another group similar to the Theatines, were also "Regular Clerks". At about the same period, the Somaschi were founded. They owe their origin to St Jerome Emiliani (1486–1537). A native of Venice, he had spent his somewhat undisciplined youth as a soldier. At the age of thirty he was miraculously delivered from the rigours of prison. He began to take stock of himself and attended the meetings of the Oratory of Divine Love at Venice. The ravages of war had caused great hardships, famine and made many children orphans. Jerome threw himself into works of charity. He had a burning love of souls. He was the first to found orphanages and he devoted all his own fortune to this work. In 1532, he set out for Verona on the invitation of the devout Bishop Giberti. He also worked at Brescia and at Bergamo. He, too, founded his Regular Clerks who took their name of Somaschi from the village in the neighbourhood of Bergamo which became their centre (1533). St Jerome Emiliani, humble, zealous, full of love for God, of confidence in Jesus Christ and of Christian optimism, is typical of the "Catholic reform" and he owes absolutely nothing to Luther. He was canonized by Clement XIII in 1767.

THE SACK OF ROME (1527)

Although the saints we have mentioned and their fervent companions owe nothing to Luther (some lived before the Protestant revolt and so have their roots in the medieval Church), yet they were affected by the repercussions of the political events which encouraged Lutheranism in its early stages. The chief of these events was the rivalry between the House of France and the House of Austria. The wars to which it gave rise took place mostly in the north of Italy. We have just seen how the Somaschi originated as a result of the calamities the wars caused. But the episode which most shocked the men of the time and had the most direct and profound influence on the "Catholic Reformation" was the sack of Rome in May 1527.

The imperial forces under the command of the Constable de Bourbon in revolt against his king, Francis I, included in their ranks some Lutheran infantry under the orders of the redoubtable Frundsberg. On May 6th, this army attacked

Rome. Bourbon was killed in battle but Rome was taken.
The Lutheran soldiers, angered by the death of their leader
before the victory, indulged in an orgy of horror in the city
of the popes. Clement VII was obliged to humble himself
before the emperor and to accept peace on conditions of the
utmost severity. The news of the sack of Rome opened the
eyes of the whole Catholic Church. It had a far greater influence on men's minds than the dissident Lutheran movement. It was interpreted as a grim warning on God's part,
a well-deserved punishment for the delay in reforming the
Church, a call to bring about the renewal of Christendom at
all costs.

We see this idea at work in the mind of Gian Matteo
Giberti. Born at Palermo in 1495, he had entered the service
of Cardinal Julian de' Medici in Rome at an early age. He
attended the meetings of the Oratory of Divine Love. He
was a friend of St Cajetan and Caraffa. When his master
became pope in 1523 as Clement VII, his secretary was
appointed bishop of Verona, but without obligation to reside.
This was a situation which could not fail to give him qualms
of conscience. In any case, he was completely unsuccessful
as a diplomat. When the thunder-clap of the sack of Rome
burst over Christendom, he was one of those who had the
clearest understanding of what it meant. He was imprisoned
by the invaders and made up his mind that he would reside
in his see as soon as he was set free. He kept his word, went
to Venice and then to Verona. He began, as everyone could
see, to work with all his strength for the reform of his diocese.
Before a year was out, an astonished observer wrote: "The
priests of this diocese cannot get over it. All of them are
being examined. The unworthy and incapable are suspended
from their functions or moved elsewhere. The prisons are
becoming full of delinquent clerks. The people are preached
to without respite. Studies are encouraged and the bishop's
own way of life is the finest example." Giberti continued
this apostolate for fifteen years until 1543 and with con-

siderable success. The recollection of what he was and did had an effective influence on the Council of Trent which met after his death. His colleagues in the episcopate—or some of them at least—imitated him as best they could. The initial impetus had been provided by him. Facts like this made the Council of Trent possible. Certain of its disciplinary decrees were taken word for word from Giberti's own reforming regulations for the Verona diocese. St Charles Borromeo, the great archbishop of Milan (1538–84) and himself a model for the bishops of the Catholic Reformation, had him constantly in his thoughts and followed in his footsteps.

THE REFORM OF THE ANCIENT ORDERS

Our description of the new Orders might suggest that the older ones had become sterile. Far from it. Blessed Paolo Giustiniani in 1520 founded the reformed Camaldolese congregation at Monte Corona near Perugia. The learned and zealous Giles of Viterbo, the general of the Augustinians, Luther's own order, was a diligent and successful reformer. The humanist Gregorio Cortese, who later became a cardinal, exercised a profound influence on the Benedictines of Monte Cassino. Among the Franciscans, a movement which had its beginnings in 1525 with Matteo de Bascio (1495–1552) was to lead to the foundation of a new branch of the Order, the Capuchins. The latter met with difficulties at first. They were on the point of being suppressed by Paul III when he learned that their general, the adventurous Bernadino Ochino, had apostatized and gone over to Protestantism. However, they survived and were to give some very great saints to the Church.

ANGELA MERICI (1474–1540)

It is clear from the dates of her birth and death that Angela Merici does not depend in any way on Luther and his re-

volt. She was therefore in the direct line of the medieval
Church. Born at Desenzano on the shores of Lake Garda, she
devoted herself at an early age to works of charity. She became a Franciscan tertiary and other young women grouped
themselves spontaneously around her. From 1516 onward
she lived at Brescia and undertook the task of educating girls.
She placed her work under the patronage of St Ursula. In
this way she founded the Ursulines who, under different forms
in Italy and in France, were to be the great women educators
of children. Their rule, approved by the bishop of Brescia in
August, 1536, was confirmed by Pope Paul III on June 9th,
1544. They were to do for girls what the Jesuits did for boys.

IGNATIUS OF LOYOLA AND THE JESUITS

The Jesuits in particular are referred to as the agents of the
"Counter-Reformation" and the representatives of a type of
religion different from that of the Middle Ages. Whether this
is really so or not we shall soon see.

The founder of the Jesuits was Ignatius of Loyola. He was
born in 1491 in the fortified castle of Loyola near Azpeitia
in Spain. His family was profoundly Catholic. He was
brought up in the customary manner of the country until his
twelfth or thirteenth year. He then became page to Juan
Velasquez de Cuellar, minister of finance to King Ferdinand
the Catholic. It was at this period that he became passionately
fond of books of chivalry, and of all things medieval. After
Velasquez's disgrace in 1517, he became gentleman in waiting
to a relative of his, the duke of Najera, viceroy of Navarre.
It was in this capacity that he directed the defence of Pam-
plona against the French and was seriously wounded on
May 20th, 1521. During his long convalescence at Loyola he
read all he could lay his hands on, and in particular, Ludolph
the Carthusian's lives of the saints and *The Life of Jesus
Christ*, translated into Castilian. He went through a period

of great mental conflict. The saints whose lives he read aroused in him an immense desire to imitate them. But it was the great saints of the Middle Ages, Francis and Dominic, who attracted him most. He chose Christ as his king and at once began thinking of going on pilgrimage to Jerusalem. Nothing could certainly have been more medieval. But before setting out he went to the famous shrine of our Lady of Montserrat. There, in the wild solitude of the rocks, he prepared for his general confession which lasted three whole days. He discarded his knight's costume, bade an interior farewell to the world and then set out to devote himself to the service of the sick at Manresa. And here he was granted so much spiritual light that he conceived the idea of and wrote his famous little book *The Spiritual Exercises*, one of the most profound and successful in the whole of ascetical and mystical literature (1522). He worked over it again and completed it at Alcala, Paris, Venice and Rome from 1522 to 1541.

After a year's stay at Manresa, he returned to his notion of a pilgrimage to Jerusalem. He arrived there in fact in September 1523. It was then that he saw he could do nothing without a thorough theological formation. Although he was now past thirty, he sat with the children on school benches and threw himself with amazing energy into the learning of Latin (1524-6). He then became a student at the Universities of Alcala and Salamanca. He began to gather disciples around him and made them read *The Spiritual Exercises,* in consequence of which he was harassed by the Inquisition and imprisoned for forty-two days at Alcala and then for twenty-two more at Salamanca. But his innocence was recognized. Nevertheless, he left Spain for Paris. The Sorbonne, so decried by Luther, was still the premier theological faculty in Christendom. Ignatius arrived there on February 2nd, 1528. He studied for seven years. He had never anything but good to say of his Alma Mater. At the Montaigu College he may have rubbed shoulders with young Calvin, eighteen years younger than himself, whose future development was to be so different from his own. There can be no doubt that at Paris Lutheranism was a continual topic of conversation and that it was opposed. Ignatius cannot have failed to join in the heated discussions on the subject at the Montaigu College. Perhaps he then conceived the idea of becoming the champion of the anti-Protestant movement, a kind of knight of the "Counter-Reformation". This is all the more likely since with his *Exercises*, which he was constantly revising and correcting, he was winning the confidence of some of his fellow-students. It was not long before seven of these bound themselves to him for life.

It is at this point that we have to ask ourselves the question: did these seven companions, only one of whom was a priest, intend to combat Protestantism? Were they "agents of a Counter-Reformation"? Not at all. Just like ordinary religious in the Middle Ages, they took the vows of poverty, chastity and obedience (those same vows Luther had denounced, condemned and vilified), but with the intention of going to Jerusalem and to work there for the conversion of the infidels. Thus they were knights in a spiritual crusade at a time when the spirit of the Crusades was quite dead. Once again, could anything be more medieval? There is no evidence that they had any anti-Protestant designs. Nor did Ignatius have any idea of founding an order. It was only later at Venice that they were to come to know the Theatines, that is, a group of Regular Clerks from whom they were to learn how it was possible for the ancient Orders to evolve, make contact with their own times and work for ecclesiastical reform. From May 1537 to May 1538, they were thinking only of going to Palestine, but there were no ships sailing there from Venice. Meanwhile, they had seen the pope, Paul III, who had questioned them and asked them to speak and discuss theological matters in his presence. He had been delighted with them. He authorized them to become priests since most of them were still not ordained. It was only then that they gave up their idea of going to Palestine and placed themselves at the pope's disposal so that he could use them as he thought fit. In 1539 they founded together the Company (Society) of Jesus. In their language, the word "company" had almost always a military sense. It is certain that from the beginning they were "militants" as we should say today. On September 3rd, 1539, Pope Paul III gave them his approval for the first time. This he did verbally. Then on September 27th, 1540, he gave them his approbation in writing in the form of a Bull. Ignatius' election as general and the first solemn profession took place at St Paul's outside the Walls on April 8th, and 22nd.

The Society began in Rome, which its members wanted to convert so that it might be no longer the scandal but the model of Catholicity. From 1541 to 1549 they spent their time giving the *Exercises*, teaching the catechism, protecting children, converting prostitutes, and leading an intensive pastoral life. They met both with success and with hostility and insults. Ignatius had founded a novitiate in which he trained his first disciples, in the strict sense of the word, in the new spirit.

The Society was limited at first by the pope to sixty members. Later this restrictive clause was lifted and it developed rapidly. It spread to Italy, Portugal, Spain and Belgium and as early as 1544 had gained a foothold in Germany at Cologne. It was there that they were mockingly called "Jesuits". They accepted this name, though at first unwillingly. Francis of Xavier (wrongly called Francis Xavier) had set out for India in 1541. He reached Goa in 1542 and began there his epic campaigns with their thousands of conversions.

After the death of Paul III, Pope Julius III in his turn gave the Society his approval on July 21st, 1550. It was only then that the aims of the institute began to take an expressly anti-Protestant direction.

In 1551 Ignatius founded the Roman College for the training of his own subjects and other ecclesiastical students from Rome and elsewhere. In 1552, he instituted the German Seminary for the training of students from Germany who were due to return to their own country. A new trend began to appear. The Society was no longer to be chiefly a missionary institute but a teaching Order. If Christian society was to be renewed it was essential to pay particular attention to the young. From 1553 to 1556 Ignatius worked on the *Constitutions*. He also founded colleges which were to have an incalculable value for the renewal in the Church, that is for the Catholic Reformation.

When Ignatius died in Rome on July 31st, 1556, he had accomplished a task few founders before him had been able to bring to a successful conclusion. To the famous *Consilium reformationis*, drawn up by a commission of cardinals by order of Paul III in 1537, he had contrived to add two essential points which had been lacking: a vigorous spirituality, powerful and organic, the spirituality of the *Exercises* which we may well describe as having a "transforming" effect; and the trend towards the education and instruction of the young, not only those destined for the priesthood but also, in a large measure, those who wanted to exert an active influence on the world while remaining in it. Like the other Regular Clerks, the Jesuits were occupied solely with apostolic work, with teaching and preaching. They had no choir obligations or special penances. But their training was long and graded, and their system of discipline placed the vow of obedience at the forefront of the religious life.

Ignatius was beatified on July 27th, 1609 and canonized on March 12th, 1622. Later we shall have something to say about the work done by the Society in the cause of reform after the Council of Trent.

CHAPTER VIII

THE COUNCIL OF TRENT

(1545–63)

TOWARDS THE COUNCIL

Although we have been able to show in the last chapter that the Church did not wait for the rebellion of Luther and his imitators before concerning herself with a very necessary reform; although it is also true that the Theatines, the Barnabites, the Somaschi, the Capuchins, the Ursulines and even the Jesuits did not owe their rise to Protestantism but were solidly rooted in medieval devotion, yet we shall admit without any difficulty that the Council of Trent was a direct result of the revolt we have described. Between Protestantism and the Council of Trent there is the same relation of cause and effect as between Arianism and the Council of Nicea, Nestorianism and the Council of Ephesus or Eutychianism and the Council of Chalcedon. But we shall not therefore agree to treat the Council of Trent as a mere Counter-Reformation movement. This would involve the admission that Protestantism was the "Reform" it claimed to be. On the contrary, the Council of Trent had no other aim but to prove that Protestantism was a corruption of Christian dogma, a heretical deviation from the historical Christian position. The Council also brought about a reform of the abuses which explained the rise of Protestantism but did not justify its errors.

We must also admit that although the "spontaneous reform" introduced by the religious Orders and the saints created a favourable atmosphere for conciliar reform, nothing final could be accomplished in the way of Catholic reform without the intervention of the Council.

Yet it was not until twenty years after Luther's revolt in 1517 and twenty-seven years after his noisy appeal to the Council that the latter could in fact be assembled. This long delay was due in the first place to the fact that Leo X could not take Luther's action seriously, and this for a very simple reason. Pius II had forbidden all such appeals. Hence Luther's move in 1518 was illegal and from a juridical point of view null and void.

After Leo X came a pope full of goodwill and zeal for reform, Adrian VI (1522-3). He had been tutor to Charles V and in his youth a disciple of the Brothers of the Common Life at Zwolle and Louvain. He was energetic, austere, rigorous even. His life was simple, devout, edifying in every way. Unfortunately he was before his time. What we have called the "climate of reform" did not yet exist. His voice was lost in the hubbub of the Lutheran revolution. He came up against the inveterate habits of the Curia and failed completely to achieve his noble ambitions. In any case, his pontificate lasted only twelve months and he was never understood by the Italian prelates who surrounded him. He was the last non-Italian pope. At the Diet of Nuremberg in 1923 Catholics and Lutherans were unanimous in calling for a Council, but their views as to the character of this Council were different. Luther wanted it to be "free", that is, held independently of the pope, and "German", that is, it was to meet in Germany where it would find an atmosphere favourable to its purposes. It was to be "Christian", that is, laymen were to be admitted on the same footing as bishops and priests.

Clement VII, Adrian VI's successor (1523-34) and like Leo X a Medici, returned to political schemes and took an active part in the formidable quarrel between the Houses of France and Austria. He suffered terribly, and doubtless by way of chastisement, as a result of the sack of Rome in 1527.

He was also worried and grieved by the affair of the English divorce, leading as it did to schism. Although his goodwill was obvious and his personal life irreproachable, his character proved too changeable, weak and irresolute, and his pontificate was unhappy and ineffective.

Paul III, a Farnese, who followed him (1534–49) was a very different man. His youth had been irregular. As pope, he still showed too much concern for his children and grandchildren, but he was obviously fully conscious of the responsibilities of his office. He wanted a Council and in spite of every opposition continued to do all he could to bring it about. To his lasting glory he succeeded. Yet the difficulties he encountered were unbelievable. Immediately after his election in 1534 he sent nuncios to France, Germany and Spain to inform their sovereigns of his plan for a Council. He convened it at Mantua for May 23rd, 1537, then in view of objections from the princes, for May 1st, 1538, and this time at Vicenza. Charles V however thought he was showing greater acumen in his "policy of conversations", that is, the convening of Congresses between Catholics and Lutherans (at Hagenau, Worms, Ratisbon, 1540–1), although this policy led nowhere. It merely served to bring more confusion to men's minds. Then there followed a new period of warfare between France and the House of Austria. It was only after the Peace of Crespy in 1544, that Paul III was able to revive his idea of a Council. On this occasion, he succeeded and the Council, after still further delays, was finally able to meet at Trent, a town considered as German, in the Tyrol, on December 13th, 1543. The history of the Council is divided into three periods: the first under Paul III (1545–49), the second under Julius III (1551–2) and the third under Pius IV (1562–3).

THE FIRST PERIOD (1545–9)

The Council was opened by the pope's legates, the cardinals del Monte (the future Julius III), Cervini (the future Marcellus II) and Pole, in the presence of the local ordinary, Cardinal Madruzzi, four archbishops, twenty-one bishops, five generals of Orders, forty-two theologians and nine doctors of Canon Law. A plan of work was first agreed upon. It was decided that only the legates should be entitled to suggest the questions to be studied and that these questions should be examined by "special congregations" of theologians and canonists. They were then to be submitted to the bishops and abbots with a right to vote in "general congregations" which were to determine what decisions were to be taken. The latter were eventually to be proclaimed in a "solemn session" in the form of doctrinal chapters and canons anathematizing errors. The emperor would have liked the assembly to confine itself to abuses and to have left dogmas aside so as not to upset the Protestants by a direct attack. This would have been a regrettable surrender of the teaching office of the Church. Thomas Campeggio, archbishop of Feltre, persuaded the Council to deal with both doctrine and disciplinary reform.

The Council first discussed the sources of Revelation. Luther had confined these sources to the Bible alone. The Council in its fourth session (April 8th, 1546) taught that the Bible (whose list of books it fixed and whose Latin translation [the Vulgate] it declared authentic whilst not excluding reference to the original languages of the Bible, Hebrew and Greek) could not abolish Tradition, that is, the writings of the Fathers, the decisions of Ecumenical Councils and the "ordinary" teaching of the Church. The Bible and Tradition were thus the Council's answer to the Protestant claim—the Bible alone.

The question of original sin, which was also a fundamental one for the Protestants, was scientifically studied and defined in the fifth session (June 17th, 1546). Luther had identified original sin with concupiscence. Hence for him baptism did not remove it. The Council on the other hand defined that baptism removes "all that offers the true and proper nature of sin".

The discussions continued unabated and faced the essential

problem of justification. It was studied for a period of six months. There were no less than forty-four "particular congregations" and sixty-one "general congregations". The draft decrees drawn up by the learned cardinals Cervini and Seripando, the general of the Augustinians, were constantly revised down to the last minute. The sixteen doctrinal chapters and the thirty-three canons were promulgated in the sixth session (January 13th, 1547). The Protestant doctrine of justification by faith alone without works was condemned on every count.

The Council then passed on to the sacraments in its seventh session (March 3rd, 1547). Luther held that there were only two. The essence of the sacraments and their number (seven) were defined in fourteen canons on the sacraments in general followed by fourteen canons on baptism and three on confirmation.

The Council was then suddenly interrupted. A conflict broke out between the pope and the emperor. Paul III, using an epidemic at Trent as a pretext, transferred the assembly to Bologna while Charles V forbade his bishops to leave Trent. At Bologna it was only possible to make preparatory studies and no doctrinal decision was taken in the eighth, ninth and tenth sessions. In 1549 the pope declared the Council suspended. He himself died on November 10th, 1549.

In accordance with the procedure that had been adopted, the Council had dealt with reform at the same time as it had worked at doctrinal questions. Its decrees in this sphere had been concerned with the scientific teaching of holy Scripture and the office of preaching (fifth session); the duty of bishops to reside in their sees, one of the most burning problems of the day (sixth session); the qualities required of a good bishop; the prohibiting of plurality of benefices; pastoral visitations, Christian hospitals, etc. (seventh session).

THE SECOND PERIOD (1551–2)

Paul III's successor was Cardinal del Monte, the first president of the Council. He took the name of Julius III. He was a man of learning, inclined to be impatient as a cardinal but who, once he became pope, showed himself gentle, peace-loving, keen upon reform but dogged by sickness (gout). One of the first things he took care to do was to reassemble the Council. To please the emperor, now rather disillusioned by his Augsburg *interim*, but still wedded to the choice of Trent as the meeting-place of the Council, the pope decided that it should once again assemble in that town. Work began again during the eleventh session (May 1st, 1551) and it was decided to return to the subject which had been studied and prepared over so long a period at Bologna, namely, the Eucharist. It was not until the thirteenth session (October 11th, 1551) that the decrees dealing with this vital matter were promulgated. Luther's doctrine of impanation and the symbolist teaching of Zwingli, Oecolampadius and Calvin were all condemned by the definition of the doctrine of transubstantiation.

The next session, the fourteenth, took place on November 25th, 1551. It defined the Catholic doctrine concerning auricular confession, the judicial character of the absolution given by the priest in the sacrament of Penance, and the necessity of making satisfaction. At the same time, the sacramental character of Extreme Unction was also defined. The reforming decrees dealt once again with the duties of bishops, the right of appeal to the pope, and the reform of the clergy in general. Then, for the first and last time, certain Protestant envoys came to the Council to ask for the suspension of the deliberations on matters of dogma until the arrival of their own theologians. Their request was granted in the hope (which proved unfounded) that it might be possible to come to an understanding with them. The Council was given a confession of faith drawn up by Brenz on behalf of Württemberg, and another, on behalf of Saxony, from the pen of Melanchthon, who after Luther's death had become the leader of the Lutheran Church at Wittenberg. But the Protestants laid down as a preliminary condition that all the decisions of the Council should be considered null and void so that discussions could begin again in their presence. Further, they demanded that the Council should be declared of superior authority to the pope.

These conditions were unacceptable. In fact, there was little time to discuss them since it was learned that the duke of Saxony, in alliance with the king of France, had risen against the emperor and the latter had been completely routed so that the Council's own safety was gravely imperilled. Hence during the twelfth session it was decided to suspend the Council (April 28th, 1552) and, in spite of the protests of the Spanish bishops, it broke up.

During 1552 and 1553 Pope Julius III attempted to make obligatory the disciplinary decrees already issued, since a certain number of Portuguese and Spanish bishops were already applying them in their dioceses on their own initiative, before they had been confirmed by the Holy See. He therefore prepared a great reforming Bull which would give juridical validity to the decisions reached at Trent. But he died on March 25th, 1555, before it had been possible for him to publish it.

His successor was Cardinal Cervini, who had been one of the legates at the Council. He took the title of Marcellus II. He was a man of great nobility of character and much was expected of him, but his pontificate only lasted twenty-two days.

He was succeeded by Giovanni Pietro Caraffa who, as we have seen, had been a close associate of St Cajetan in the foundation of the Theatines. He took the name of Paul IV. He was an impetuous Neapolitan, born at Capriglio in 1476, a man of energy, authoritarian, devout and ascetic in his personal life, but somewhat abrupt and filled with suspicion of Spaniards, especially of Charles V and still more of his son Philip II.

In his view, the Council, whose progress had been continually slowed down by interventions on the part of the emperor and the monarchs of Spain and France, was not making the necessary reforming decisions quickly enough.

He intended to assemble in Rome a reforming Commission on which he could keep his eye so that it would act with greater promptitude. The Council would then have merely to confirm the decisions taken. But involved as he was in an unfortunate struggle with Spain and compromised by scandals caused by his own family, this excellent pope died in 1559 without having done anything he had desired to do. He only succeeded in making himself very unpopular because of his severity.

It was his successor, Pius IV (Giovanni-Angelo Medici of Milan and no relation to the Medicis of Florence) who deserves the credit for reopening the Council and bringing it to a successful conclusion.

THE THIRD PERIOD (1562–3)

In the Bull *Ad Ecclesiae regimen*, Pius IV, admirably assisted by his young nephew, Charles Borromeo, whom he had appointed his "secretary of State", called the Council together, again at Trent, on November 29th, 1560. The political situation was hardly favourable. In Germany, the Peace of Augsburg in 1555 had given legal recognition to the Lutherans on the same footing as the Catholics. The invitation to the Council was taken to Germany by Cardinals Delfino and Commendone. The Lutheran princes, assembled at Naumburg from January 20th to February 6th, 1561, rudely repulsed the advances of the Holy See. The Catholic princes, intimidated by the threatening attitude of the Lutherans, showed little eagerness to go to Trent. But the principal opposition came from France. King Henry II had died a tragic death in 1559. Under King Francis II, a young and sickly monarch, the Guise family had assumed effective power. But Francis II had also died and during the minority of Charles IX, his mother, Catherine de' Medici, had every intention of exercising her powers as regent. She was hostile to the General Council and claimed that she could direct the affairs of her kingdom by means of a "discussion", which took place in fact at Poissy (August–September, 1561) but without the slightest result. At Rome, it was even feared that there would be a Gallican schism. In spite of all these difficulties Pius IV sent his legates to Trent, Cardinals Seripando, Hosius, Simonetta and Hohenems. The first three were excellent men, the last, one of the pope's nephews, was quite insignificant.

It was not until January 18th, 1562, that the Council could begin work in its seventeenth session. It established the principle, though with some difficulty, that it was continuing the sessions which had been interrupted ten years previously, and so was not a new Council. But as the emperor, Ferdinand I, for fear of the Protestants, had been opposed to the restatement of the doctrinal decisions which were to deal with the sacrifice of the Mass, a doctrine so violently rejected by Protestantism, the Council confined itself to completing its work on the Index of prohibited books during its eighteenth session (February 26th, 1562). Then followed a fierce discussion on the problem which had already on so many occasions proved a bone of contention between the bishops themselves, namely, their obligation to reside in their sees. The point at issue was whether this duty was imposed by divine or by ecclesiastical law. A minority made up of the Spanish and some imperial bishops, together with a few Italians, maintained that it was a question of divine law since the episcopate itself was *de jure divino*, so that neither the pope nor a General Council could abolish bishops in the Church. The majority, while agreeing on this point, considered that the duty to reside, if held to be *de jure divino*, would limit papal jurisdiction, since the pope could keep his bishops subject to his primacy either in Rome or send them on pontifical missions. The legates themselves were divided. Seripando and Cardinal Gonzaga sided with the minority, Simonetta with the majority. The pope reprimanded the former and ordered the whole question to be postponed till later. A serious crisis then arose in the Council itself. Thus sessions nineteen (May 14th) and twenty (June 5th, 1562) were fruitless.

The Council began work again on June 6th. Cardinal Gonzaga made a declaration postponing the problem of episcopal residence until discussion took place on the sacrament of Holy Orders.

During the twenty-first session (July 16th, 1562) it was decreed that communion under both kinds was in no way essential. A little later it was agreed to refer to the pope the question of *permitting* communion under both kinds since both the emperor and the duke of Bavaria had asked this to be permitted. In fact, the concession was granted but it gave rise to so much inconvenience that those who availed themselves of it soon gave it up.

The twenty-second session on September 17th, 1562 was one of the most important. It dealt with the Mass which was defined as a true sacrifice applicable to the dead and able to be celebrated in honour of the saints.

Meanwhile, reforming decrees had been voted. But there was a great deal of uneasiness among those present, for many bishops, in particular the Spaniards, considered that the Council, doubtless held in check by the pope, was not going far enough. The opposition grew suddenly much larger by the very late arrival at the Council of the French bishops under the leadership of the Cardinal of Lorraine (Charles de Guise). They immediately joined the minority. For a short time it looked as though the Council was on the point of disbanding. The crisis was at its height when Cardinal Gonzaga died on March 2nd, 1563. On March 17th, he was followed to the grave by Cardinal Seripando. The pope, in a personal letter to Philip II, succeeded in convincing him that he wished to correct all abuses and to undertake a fundamental reform (April 1st, 1653). He then appointed two new legates: Cardinals Giovanni Morone and Bernardo Navagero. The former especially was a first-class diplomat.

He took action without delay, went to see the emperor at Innsbruck, convinced him and also won over the Cardinal of Lorraine. The Council was saved. In the twenty-third session (July 15th, 1563), the sacrament of Holy Orders received masterly treatment. The duty of episcopal residence was asserted without any final decision in either sense regarding the question of the divine law. But more important than all the rest for the future of the Church was article 18, which attracted little attention at the time. It took its lead from a decree of Cardinal Pole intended to be applied in England. It was laid down that all the bishops were to establish seminaries for the training of their clergy. It has been well said that, if the Council had done nothing else, this regulation would have justified its activities. The benefits which were to emerge for the Church in the course of time, although not envisaged at the outset, have in fact proved incalculable. For any impartial observer, it is the training of the clergy in the seminaries which forms the vital centre of Catholic life. Nothing is more important than to maintain the seminaries in contact with the needs of the times. They must never be allowed to become bogged down in the routine of the past, nor must they lose themselves in the utopias of the present or the future.

The final sessions of the Council (the twenty-fourth, November 11th, 1563, and the twenty-fifth, December 3rd–4th, 1563) dealt, the first with Christian marriage on which it issued the decree *Tametsi*, declaring clandestine marriage invalid, any marriage, that is, which was not entered into in the presence of the parish priest and two witnesses; and the second with purgatory, the veneration of the saints, and relics.

Session twenty-five had been put forward ten days because the pope was reported to be gravely ill. At the end of the Council, the Cardinal of Lorraine, who was one of its most eminent members, made a speech in which he loudly praised the pope, the emperor and all those who had promoted the Council. Then, the Council's secretary, Angelo Massarelli, who had held this office from the very beginning in 1545, asked all the Fathers to sign. There were present 199 bishops or archbishops, seven abbots, seven generals of Orders and nineteen procurators acting for prelates who were absent.

If we are to realize what the results that had been obtained really were in the opinion of contemporaries, we should re-read the speech of Bishop Ragazzoni which brought the Council to its close:

> Henceforth, ambition will no longer take the place of virtue in the sacred ministry. The word of the Lord will be preached more frequently and more carefully. The bishops will remain among their flocks. Henceforth, there will be no more privileges to cover up vice and error, no more indigent or idle priests. Holy things will no more be bought and sold and we shall see no more the scandalous traffic of professional beggars. Ministers who have been brought up from childhood to serve the Lord will be taught to offer him a purer and more worthy worship. Provincial synods will be re-established, strict rules laid down for the conferring of the cure of souls and of benefices. It will be forbidden to hand on Church goods as though they were an inheritance. The weapon of excommunication will be more strictly controlled, a powerful brake put upon cupidity, licence and luxury in the case of both ecclesiastics and laymen, wise advice will be given to kings and the great ones of the earth. Is not all this enough to show what great and holy things you have accomplished?

It is noteworthy that this speech contains an official avowal of past abuses as well as a list of the reforms effected by the Council. It is true, of course, that there were to be many deplorable departures from its regulations in the future, but, taken as a whole, the speaker's statements were correct.

We must also insist that side by side with its disciplinary reforms, the dogmatic work of the Council was equally important. Over against the "variations" of Protestantism, it offered the majestic unity of Catholic dogma and served as a solid foundation and as a point of departure for the later speculations of theology, particularly as regards grace. In our next chapter we shall see the Catholic Reformation in full flower after the Council.

CHAPTER IX

THE CATHOLIC REFORMATION AFTER THE COUNCIL OF TRENT (1563–1623)

THE POPES

The papacy had wanted the Council, the papacy had brought it to a successful conclusion, it was to the papacy that it owed its success. We must therefore glance briefly at the popes who reigned after the Council, without going into any details concerning their history which, by force of circumstances, was always more or less involved in politics, but in order to note what they achieved for the Catholic Reformation along the lines laid down by the Council.

Pius IV lived long enough to confirm unconditionally, with the help of his admirable nephew, Charles Borromeo, the Council's decisions, as early as January 26th, 1564. He was also able to execute its decrees, particularly by establishing a Roman Seminary and several in the Milan diocese whose archbishop was Charles Borromeo (1564–5). On August 2nd, 1564, the pope entrusted a commission of cardinals with the task of seeing that the Council's decrees were applied throughout the Church. This commission was later to become the Sacred Congregation of the Council. On March 24th, the

Index of prohibited books prescribed by the Council had already been published. On November 13th, 1546, a *Professio Fidei* was made obligatory on all in possession of benefices with the cure of souls, namely, all bishops and parish priests. When the pope died on December 9th, 1565, the impetus had been given to the Tridentine reform in all the countries which had accepted the Council: Italy, Spain, Portugal, Poland (but not France or Austria).

Pius IV was succeeded by Cardinal Michele Ghislieri, a Dominican who took the name Pius V. His election on January 7th, 1566, surprised everybody. There could not have been a better choice. Pius V was a saint. He bent all his energies to continuing the work of his predecessor. The importance, vigour and far-reaching nature of his work are his distinguishing feature. He sent the Council's decrees to all the bishops, including those of Goa, Mexico and Venezuela. He made in person a canonical visitation of his own diocese of Rome, sent apostolic visitors to all the dioceses in the papal States, in the kingdom of Naples and in Upper Italy. There were reforming diocesan and provincial synods, at Milan in particular where Charles Borromeo, its archbishop, had been in residence since the death of his uncle. It was Pius V who issued the Roman Catechism in 1568, the reformed Roman Breviary in 1568 and the Roman Missal in 1570. He proclaimed Thomas Aquinas a doctor of the Church on April 11th, 1567. On October 1st of the same year he condemned seventy-nine propositions from the works of Michael Baius, the forerunner of Jansenism.

He was less successful in England where he had to excommunicate Elizabeth on February 25th, 1570. One of the most glorious events of his pontificate was the victory of Lepanto (October 7th, 1571) which broke the Ottoman power. This pope died on May 1st, 1572. He was beatified by Clement X in 1672 and canonized by Clement XI in 1712.

After him, Gregory XIII (Ugo Boncompagni) ruled the Church from 1572 to 1585. Although over seventy at the time of his election to the chair of St Peter, he was admirably active, always in the cause of reform. He was helped by the example of Charles Borromeo, the model bishop of those days, and by the advice and prayers of St Philip Neri. He founded or took under his protection twenty-three seminaries, manned by Jesuits, and gave his name to the famous Gregorian University in Rome where so many experts in Catholic doctrine have been trained down to our own days. He too condemned Baius, but was successful in obtaining his complete submission. He must be judged one of the finest popes of the modern era and one of the most active in the cause of reform.

His successor was a Franciscan, a man of very humble origins, who took the title of Sixtus V (1585–90). He was known as Sixtus the Terrible. He was in fact a man of indomitable energy and an authoritarian and stern pope. It was he who limited the number of the cardinals to seventy (1586). This arrangement was to remain unchanged until the pontificate of John XXIII. He gave their final form to the Roman Congregations. They were fifteen in number, nine for spiritual and six for temporal purposes (1588). He showed the greatest possible energy in the repression of brigandage in the papal states. It had become so widespread that, in order to abolish it, it was necessary to fight a pitched battle against a band of over 800 brigands. Like his predecessor, he gave powerful support to foreign missions which were very active at the time in the Philippines, Japan and Latin America.

After the brief pontificate of Urban VII which only lasted from September 15th to September 27th, 1590, Gregory XIV proved a zealous and exemplary pope but he only reigned for ten months and ten days. His successor, Innocent IX, had an even shorter pontificate. He was pope from October 29th to December 30th, 1591.

Clement VIII, who reigned from 1592 to 1605, was a brilliant and successful pontiff. He was a reformer like his predecessors whom we have just named. He issued a revised version of the Vulgate and so continued an enterprise which had been attempted but without success by Sixtus V. He published new editions of the liturgical books, the Breviary and the Missal, and revised the Index which was brought up to date. It is to his credit that he appointed cardinals of the highest quality such as Baronius, Bellarmine, Tolet and Duperron. It was he who gave solemn absolution to Henry IV, king of France, after the latter's conversion in 1593. This act gave free play to a constructive reign which France badly needed. One of the most interesting events in his pontificate was the setting up of the *De Auxiliis* Congregation in 1596. It was intended to come to a decision in the discussions between the Jesuits (especially Molina) and the Dominicans (especially Bañez) on the subject of grace and predestination. The pope decided that he would take part personally in the argument; it lasted for ten years (1598–1607) but without reaching any conclusion.

After the twenty-six days of Leo XI's pontificate, Camillo Borghese became pope and took the name Paul V (1605–21). He took great pride in the fact that he had completed the building of St Peter's which had been in progress for more than a century. He also brought the work of the *De Auxiliis* Congregation to an end. To him goes the credit above all of giving approval to new congregations, such as the Oratorians of Philip Neri and Bérulle, the Piarists or Regular Clerks of the Mother of God (Giovanni Leonardi) and the Visitandines of Francis of Sales and Jeanne de Chantal. On the debit side, he has been blamed for excessive nepotism. It is a fact that the wealth of the Borghese family dates from his pontificate.

We end this list of popes with Gregory XV whose pontificate lasted only two years (1621–3). It was the most fruitful of the shorter reigns. Gregory was the first pupil of the Jesuits to become pope. Together with them, he did an immense amount of work. He canonized on the same day, March 12th,

1622, two founders of Orders, Ignatius of Loyola and Philip Neri, a famous apostle, Francis of Xavier, Teresa of Avila, an incomparable reformer, and with them a simple, obscure Spanish peasant, St Isidore, who had lived in the thirteenth century. It was Gregory XV also who beatified Peter of Alcantara and Albert the Great. Finally, he founded Propaganda, the Congregation especially responsible for foreign missions (January 6th, 1622).

SAINTLY BISHOPS

It has been possible to name all the popes from 1563 to 1623, but we cannot list all the excellent bishops who brought about the Catholic Reformation during this same period. We must however give an account of a few of them.

As we know, the most exemplary was Charles Borromeo (1538–84). We have already seen him at his post of secretary of state. He was the first to occupy this position and he held it during the reign of his uncle, Pius IV. The diocese of Milan, the scene of his zealous activity for eighteen years after his uncle's death, was immense. It extended over and beyond Lombardy to parts of Venetia, Switzerland and the State of Genoa. And it had fifteen suffragan bishoprics. Charles Borromeo showed incredible industry in the application of the Council's decrees. He called on the assistance of the new congregations, the Jesuits, Barnabites, Theatines and Ursulines. He went even further and grouped the best of his priests into a new society, the Oblates of St Ambrose who later became known as the Oblates of St Charles. He held no less than eleven diocesan and five provincial synods. But above all he set an example by his personal life of zeal, penance, prayer and pastoral activity. He visited even the most distant parishes in the mountains, looked into everything and set everything in order. The plague of 1576 provided him with a never-to-be-forgotten opportunity of showing his immense charity. Eleven years after his death, he was to have

as one of his successors the celebrated Cardinal Frederigo
Borromeo, a fervent follower of his example and founder of
the superb Ambrosian Library and the Ambrosian Picture
Gallery. He was one of the most respected and charitable
prelates of his day (died 1631).

Another of the most saintly bishops of the time and one
of the great names in the history of the French language, St
Francis de Sales (1567–1622), also followed in the footsteps
of Charles Borromeo. He is the author of *Introduction to
the Devout Life*, whose essential aim is to prove that devotion,
that is, true Christian piety, is compatible with every state
of life and can be practised even in the midst of worldly
cares. But St Francis de Sales was also a very great mystic.
He wrote a magnificent book entitled *A Treatise on the
Love of God*. One of his fellow-workers was Jeanne de Chantal, an admirable personality, who was to live for a further
nineteen years after his death. He had entrusted her to the
spiritual care of another saint of the first rank, Vincent de
Paul, whose life, so full of good works, began in the time of
the popes already mentioned but in fact belongs to the next
period.

When we remember that Francis de Sales, in spite of his
zeal and his efforts, could not found a seminary in his diocese,
we may gain some idea of the difficulty of this undertaking,
and we are naturally inclined to place among the number of
excellent bishops those who were the first to bring it to a
successful conclusion.

We have seen that the first seminaries after the German
College founded in 1552 by St Ignatius Loyola, were those
of Rome and Milan. These were followed by the seminaries
of Eichstätt (1546), Wurzburg (1570), Breslau (1571), Trent
(1580), Salzburg (1582), Münster (1610) and Cologne (1615).
France was only to join in the movement much later, in the
seventeenth century. In Italy, there were a few less spectacular
successes at Rieti, Larino, Camerino and Montepulciano.

THE SAINTS

Beside popes and bishops, the saints, by their activities after the Council of Trent, also provided proof that something had changed in the Church. We cannot mention them all nor give a biography of each. We can only name a few who were especially active and successful. In the front rank must be placed Philip Neri.

He was a Florentine and born as far back as 1515. He was intended for a commercial career. He toyed with it for a time and then felt that his vocation lay elsewhere. He was attracted to charitable works and theological studies. In 1548, he founded in Rome the Confraternity of the Holy Trinity whose purpose was to welcome and lodge poor pilgrims. He gathered helpers around him and ten years later founded the huge hospice of the Holy Trinity. In the meantime, in 1551, he had become a priest. It was then that he conceived the idea of giving spiritual exercises of his own devising. He did so at first in his own room at the priests' house at St Jerome's which was itself an offshoot of St Cajetan's Oratory of Divine Love. Soon Philip too was to have his own Oratory. People came from all over the city to hear him and to take part with him in a service of adoration accompanied by sacred music carefully rehearsed. This type of music was later to be known as "Oratorio" although at the outset it had been of a thoroughly popular kind. From this period onward, Philip undertook an apostolate which bore amazing fruit in the city of the popes. He is the "happy" saint *par excellence*. Whereas Calvin's puritanism was somewhat sombre, sad and tense, Philip's was steeped in joy. And he was able to adapt himself to any company and to everyone he met. He could share in the children's games as well as in the theologians' discussions and in the deliberations of great prelates or even of popes. He had a special gift for the conversion of sinners. He was joined by other priests and in 1564 founded a new congregation with its headquarters at Santa Maria in Vallicella. One of his most remarkable recruits was the future Cardinal Baronius who was to succeed him as superior of the Oratory and who in 1568 began his *Ecclesiastical Annals*. It was a reply (on the same lines but on a vaster scale than that of St Peter Canisius) to the Centuriators of Magdeburg, Protestant historians whose leading spirit was Flacius Illyricus. They had undertaken to vilify the Church by writing her history according to their own ideas.

The founder of the Oratory died at the age of eighty on May 22nd, 1595. His was the memory most venerated and loved in Rome and throughout Italy. The French Oratory under Bérulle was to be a replica of its Roman model and, like it, to combine devotion with learning.

Camillus of Lellis, born in the Abruzzi in 1550, was first a soldier, an adventurer and a gambler. He was converted in 1575, and became a Capuchin and a follower of Philip Neri, whose influence was clearly to be found everywhere. In 1584, he began to consider the possibility of founding a religious society devoted to the care of the sick. On September 5th in the same year, he obtained approval from Pope Sixtus V for his "Ministers of the Sick" who took as their headquarters the house and Church of St Mary Magdalen in Rome. It was there that Camillus and his twenty-five companions made their religious profession. To the three usual vows was added another pledging assistance to the sick even in time of plague. Gregory XIV erected them into a Congregation of Regular Clerks, the Camillans. Their founder, who died in 1614, was canonized by Benedict XIV and proclaimed "Protector of all male Nurses" by Pius XI in 1930, a proof that we still are indebted to these saintly heroes of the sixteenth century.

Nor must we forget the three young saints so often held up as objects to be admired and imitated by Catholic youth. Stanislas Kotska (1550–68), St Aloysius Gonzaga, his rival in purity and fervour (1568–91) and St John Berchmans

whose own saintly life was due to their example (1599–1625).
All three were Jesuits.

Then there are: Francis Borgia (1510–72), a former duke of
Gandia, and afterwards a humble religious and the third
general of the Society of Jesus. He restored the honour of the
family name which had been dragged in the dust by a pope;
St Robert Bellarmine (1542–1621), a very great theologian,
adviser to popes, author of works of immense erudition, and,
as archbishop of Capua, a rival of the saintly bishops we
have already mentioned. Finally there is St Peter Canisius
(1521–97), who has been proclaimed a doctor of the Church
as has Bellarmine. He was one of the most successful workers
for the revival of the Catholic Church, so successful indeed
that he has been called the "second apostle of Germany". He
was the author of a Catechism which was so widely used that
it was for a long time the custom in Germany to ask a child
not "Do you know your Catechism?" but "Do you know your
Canisius?" He was not only learned but unfailingly kind,
broadminded, indulgent and gentle. Even his opponents could
not help recognizing these qualities in him. But over and
above the canonized saints, there were numbers of worthy
and devout religious such as Fr Skarga in Poland (1536–1612)
and Fr Auger (1530–91), one of the most remarkable French
Jesuits of the period.

Before we pass on to Spain, where we shall find saints of the
highest rank, there are two more in Italy whom we must
mention: Catherine de Ricci (1552–90), a Dominican nun,
born in Florence and brought up to admire Savonarola (and
this she continued to do in spite of everything), in close touch
with Philip Neri where spiritual matters were concerned, and
also with St Pius V, Charles Borromeo and St Mary Magdalen dei Pazzi (whom we shall also mention) and favoured with
mystical gifts of the highest order: Mary Magdalen dei Pazzi
(1566–1607), daughter of a famous Florentine family who
were rivals of the Medicis, became a Carmelite at St Mary

of the Angels in Florence and proved herself devoted to Catholic reform and lived her life hidden with Christ in God.

The list grows longer and still more glorious when we pass to Spain. Of all the Catholic countries, Spain was least affected by Protestantism and most attached to the great medieval tradition. The Catholic Reformation had begun there before the days of Luther. It owed its inception to the famous Cardinal Diego Ximenes de Cisneros (died 1517), a powerful agent in the restoration of learning, founder of the University of Alcala, which was to rival Salamanca, originator of the polyglot Bible (six folio volumes, 1514–17), at the very moment when Luther was insisting that the Church had forgotten the Bible.

Among the Spanish saints of the period we may mention St John of Sahagun (1429–79), Blessed John of Avila (1499 [or 1500]–1569), the tireless reformer of Andalusia and author of a delightful book *Audi, Filia*; St John of God (1495–1550) whose principal centre of operations was Granada. He founded a Congregation which continues its active work in our own day, and devotes itself to the care of the mentally ill. To these must be added the name of Blessed John Grande (1546–1600) who called himself "the Sinner". He spent his life in the service of the sick in hospitals as a member of the Congregation of St John of God and died in 1600, a victim of the plague, whose ravages in Andalusia he had done his best to stop.

We now pass on to the greatest figures in the history of Catholic mysticism: St Peter of Alcantara (1499–1562), Franciscan, an outstanding reformer of his Order and spiritual director of the great Teresa of Avila (1515–82), the reformer of Carmel, foundress of seventeen convents obeying the Rule she had restored, not to mention the fifteen houses of Discalced Carmelite friars who owed their existence to St John of the Cross (1542–91).

THE FOREIGN MISSIONS

While the list of saints who lived before, during and after the immediate period of the Council of Trent is an admirable one, while we find in it one proof of the power of the reform movement which gripped the Church in the sixteenth century, there is another no less striking. It is to be found in the expansion of the missions which gave to the Church converts from non-Christian lands in sufficient numbers to counterbalance her losses in the dissident Protestant countries.

As we think of the missions in those days, one name comes at once to mind, that of Francis of Xavier (1506–52). He was in fact the most amazing missionary of modern times. The soundest research attributes to him no less than 30,000 conversions of non-Christians in India and even as far as Japan. This number has sometimes been grossly exaggerated. But we should be wrong to date Catholic missionary expansion from his work. We may also note in passing that neither Luther nor Calvin, nor any other dissident "reformer" ever thought of working for the conversion of non-Christians. Once they had decided that the Church was corrupt, they worked solely to pervert Catholics and considered that pagans and Jews were victims of God's eternal decree of reprobation. (But in all honesty, we must make it clear that subsequently Protestants rediscovered the missionary spirit, and to such good purpose that they now spend more money on missions to non-Christians than do Catholics.)

Catholic missionary expansion on the contrary was intensive once the great maritime discoveries of bold Portuguese and Spanish navigators such as Diaz, Vasco da Gama, Magellan and Christopher Columbus, a Genoese in the service of Spain, had opened new paths for the spread of the Gospel. Unfortunately there was then, as always down to our own days, a certain opposition between the ambitions, conduct and vices of the conquerors on the one hand and the missionaries of Christianity on the other. Before Francis of Xavier, all the old Orders, Franciscans, Dominicans, Augustinians, Hieronymites and others, had thrown themselves into this magnificent apostolic undertaking. They were to be found in the Congo, in India, in Japan and above all in America. The first coloured bishop was consecrated, not in our own times, but in 1518. He was a native of the Congo. In America the *conquistadores* were always accompanied by missionaries who often had to oppose their methods of conquest and colonization. The most famous of the defenders of the rights of the natives against the exactions of the white men was, as is well known, Bartolome de las Casas, a Dominican (1474–1566). If we outline his career, we shall be giving a summary of those of the majority of his colleagues. Born at Seville in 1474, he studied at Salamanca and immediately became interested in the great discoveries of his time. His father, it should be remembered, had been with Christopher Columbus during his second voyage in 1493. At the age of twenty-eight he himself set out for Hispaniola, the name given by Columbus to Haiti, and he there took possession of the rich "fazenda" he had inherited from his father. He began therefore by being an exploiter of the Indians. He records the fact with profound regret in his *History of the Indies*. But he came into contact with some Dominican missionaries, was converted, and became a secular priest in 1510 and a Dominican in 1523. Already at a much earlier date he had admitted the frightful abuses perpetrated by the *encomienda*, namely, the shameless exploitation of the Indians in the colonies, and he had become the natives' advocate. He crossed the ocean a dozen times to plead their cause before Charles V. In 1539 he wrote his *Brief Account of the Destruction of the Indies*, a poignant book which was not printed at Seville until 1542. It was then translated into several languages. From 1542 onward, there was a series of new laws promulgated by Charles V in favour of the oppressed Indians. De las Casas was appointed by him bishop of Chiapa in what is now Mexico. His consecration took place at Seville on March 30th,

1544. But he was shockingly treated by the oppressors of the Indians who accused him of treason and heresy and so forced him to return to Spain where he continued his literary activities in writings not all of which have been published. Eventually in 1566 he died at Madrid at the age of ninety-two. Although we agree that he may sometimes have painted too dark a picture of the abuses of colonization, we have to admit that he fought for the honour of the Catholic cause against the excesses of commercialism.

His protests had not been in vain, for another Dominican, Louis Bertrand, born at Valence in 1526, wished to become a missionary when he heard of the great ill-usage to which the wretched Indians were subjected. He became a religious in 1544 and a priest in 1547. He set out for America and reached New Granada (Columbia) in 1562. He became its apostle, converted thousands of the natives, worked numerous miracles, and devoted himself to the defence of his beloved Indians. But seven years later, unable any longer to endure the horrors of Spanish domination, he returned to Valence, preached there, performed miracles, set an example of penitence and died in 1581. He was beatified by Paul V in 1608 and canonized by Clement X in 1671.

The latter also canonized on the same day the delightful St Rose of Lima, the "flower of America", who died at the age of thirty-one in Peru (1617). She was a Dominican Tertiary and remarkable for her admirable spirit of penitence and prayer and for her mystical graces.

It is impossible to mention Lima without referring to the saintly archbishop Alfonso Mogrovejo Toribio, born at Majorca in 1538. He was a great reformer of abuses in his diocese of Lima, held numerous synods and never tired of making pastoral visitations. He founded seminaries, churches, hospitals and died at Santa during his third visitation of his enormous diocese, on March 23rd, 1606. In his lifetime he had won large numbers of Indians to the faith.

And we end this list of saints with Francis of Solano (1549–

1610), a Spanish Franciscan. He too was a great converter of Indians, first in Tucuman, then in Argentina and finally in Peru.

In South America and the West Indies, the natives who became Christians could be counted by the million in those days. There can be no doubt that missionary expansion in the sixteenth century was an epic of incomparable grandeur, especially if we bear in mind the length, the perils and the difficulties of every kind of journey by sea or land, as well as the privations and exhaustion which the apostles of Jesus Christ accepted so that the Cross might triumph in the most distant regions of the earth.

SELECT BIBLIOGRAPHY

In this series: CRISTIANI, Léon: *Heresies and Heretics*; DVORNIK, Francis: *The General Councils of the Church*; GUILLEMAIN, Bernard: *The Later Middle Ages*; ORMESSON, Wladimir d': *The Papacy*; TAVARD, George H.: *Protestantism.*

AUCLAIR, Marcelle: *Saint Teresa of Avila*, London, Burns and Oates, and New York, Pantheon, 1953.

BREMOND, Henri: *Literary History of Religious Thought in France*, three volumes, London, S.P.C.K., and New York, Macmillan, 1929–37.

BRODRICK, James, S.J.: *St Ignatius Loyola: The Pilgrim Years*, London, Burns and Oates, and New York, Farrar, Strauss, 1956; *Origin of the Jesuits*, London and New York, Longmans, 1940; *Progress of the Jesuits*, London and New York, Longmans, 1947.

BRUNO DE JÉSUS MARIE, O.C.D.: *St John of the Cross*, London and New York, Sheed and Ward, 1936.

Cambridge Economic History of Europe, The, two volumes, Cambridge and New York, Cambridge Univ. Press, 1941–52.

FLICK, A. C.: *The Decline of the Medieval Church*, London, Kegan Paul, 1930.

HUGHES, Philip: *The Reformation in England*, three volumes, London, Hollis and Carter, and New York, Macmillan, 1950–4; *A Popular History of the Reformation*, London, Hollis and Carter, and New York, Doubleday, 1957; *A History of the Church*: volume III, *The Revolt against the Church: Aquinas to Luther*, London and New York, Sheed and Ward, 1947; *The Church in Crisis*, London, Burns and Oates, and New York, Doubleday, 1961.

KNOX, R. A.: *Enthusiasm*, London and New York, Oxford Univ. Press, 1950.

Oxford History of Modern Europe, London and New York, Oxford Univ. Press, 1954.

PASTOR, Ludwig von: *The History of the Popes from the Close of the Middle Ages*, forty volumes, London, Kegan Paul, and St Louis, Herder, 1927–40.

POURRAT, Pierre: *Christian Spirituality*, volume III, London, Burns and Oates, 1923, and Westminster, Md, Newman Press, 1953.